SPECTRUM

Language Arts

Grade 6

Columbus, Ohio

Author

Dr. Betty Jane Wagner

Professor
Reading and Language Department
National-Louis University
Evanston, IL

Editorial Reviewer Board

Illustration
Steve McInturff

School Specialty
Children's Publishing

Copyright © 2002 School Specialty Children's Publishing. Published by Spectrum, an imprint of School Specialty Children's Publishing, a member of the School Specialty Family.

Send all inquiries to:
School Specialty Children's Publishing
8720 Orion Place
Columbus, OH 43240-2111

ISBN 1-57768-486-9

4 5 6 7 8 9 10 11 VHG 09 08 07 06 05 04

Table of Contents

Mechanics ....

Capitalization
        pages

Lesson 1   Sentences, Titles, Days, Months, People 2-3

Lesson 2   Places, Documents, Groups 4-5

Lesson 3   Titles 6-7

Lesson 4   Direct Quotations 8-9

Lesson 5   Friendly and Business Letters 10-11

Lesson 6   Review: Capitalization 12-13

Punctuation

Lesson 7   Sentences, Abbreviations, and Initials 14-15

Lesson 8   Other Abbreviations 16-17

Lesson 9   End Marks 18-19

Lesson 10   Sentences 20-21

Lesson 11   Sentence Fragments 22-23

Lesson 12   Review: Punctuation 24-25

Lesson 13   Commas 26-27

Lesson 14   Commas After Phrases and Clauses 28-29

Lesson 15   Semicolons and Colons 30-31

Lesson 16   Review: Commas, Colons, Semicolons 32-33

Lesson 17   Dialogue—Commas and End Marks 34-35

Lesson 18   Direct and Indirect Quotations 36-37

Lesson 19   Friendly and Business Letters 38-39

Lesson 20   Review: Punctuation 40-41

Usage ....

Using the Appropriate Word
        pages

Lesson 21   Verbs—Froze, Shook, Rang 42-43

Lesson 22   Verbs—Swam, Tore, Took 44-45

Lesson 23   Verbs—Wrote, Stole, Began 46-47

Lesson 24   Verbs—Blew, Sank, Fell 48-49

Lesson 25   Verbs—Lie/Lay, Rise/Raise 50-51

Lesson 26   Verbs—Can/May, Let/Leave, Teach/Learn, Bring/Take 52-53

Lesson 27   Review: Verbs 54-55

Lesson 28   Adjectives 56-57

Lesson 29   Adverbs 58-59

Lesson 30   Good/Well, Bad/Badly 60-61

Lesson 31   Accept/Except, Loose/Lose, Than/Then..............................62-63
Lesson 32   Principle/Principal, There/They're/Their, Its/It's................64-65
Lesson 33   Review: Adjectives, Adverbs..66-67

Special Problems

Lesson 34   Plural Nouns...68-69
Lesson 35   Possessive Nouns...70-71
Lesson 36   Contractions..72-73
Lesson 37   Review: Plurals, Possessives, Contractions........................74-75
Lesson 38   Simple Past Tense..76-77
Lesson 39   Subject-Verb Agreement I...78-79
Lesson 40   Subject-Verb Agreement II..80-81
Lesson 41   Review: Past Tense Verbs, Subject-Verb Agreement..............82-83
Lesson 42   Pronouns—Agreement and Order I....................................84-85
Lesson 43   Pronouns—Agreement and Order II...................................86-87
Lesson 44   Double Negatives...88-89
Lesson 45   Review: Pronoun Agreement and Double Negatives.............90-91

Grammar...

Parts of Speech   pages

Lesson 46   Nouns..92-93
Lesson 47   Pronouns..94-95
Lesson 48   Verbs..96-97
Lesson 49   Irregular Verbs...98-99
Lesson 50   Adjectives...100-101
Lesson 51   Articles..102-103
Lesson 52   Adverbs..104-105
Lesson 53   Conjunctions and Interjections......................................106-107
Lesson 54   Prepositions...108-109
Lesson 55   Review: Parts of Speech...110-111

Sentences

Lesson 56   Combining Sentences I..112-113
Lesson 57   Combining Sentences II...114-115
Lesson 58   Combining Sentences III..116-117
Lesson 59   Combining Sentences IV..118-119
Lesson 60   Review: Understanding and Combining Sentences.............120-121

Answer Key...122-151

iv

Proofreading Marks

lowercase: / $\cancel{S}$ister

capitalize: ≡ o̲h̲i̲o̲

delete: ℓ ~~word~~

transpose: ∿ sheeps᷉ wool

insert: ∧ a ∧sunset
              beautiful

add... a comma: ⌃

a period: ⊙

a colon: ⌃

a semicolon: ⌃

a quotation mark: ⌄

an apostrophe: ⌄

1

1 Capitalization: Sentences, Titles, Days, Months, People

✏️ *To capitalize or not to capitalize? Writers need to know how to answer this question about the words they write.*

·····················Did You Know?·····················

The first word of a sentence is capitalized.

> **P**lease sign your name on the line at the bottom.

The names of people and pets are capitalized. So are people's initials and titles.

> **D**avid **J**acobson   **B**uck   **M**r. **A**lfonso **G**arcia, **J**r.

Words used to name relatives are capitalized *only* when the words are used as names or as part of names. They are not capitalized when preceded by a possessive pronoun, such as *my, your,* or *his*.

> Will **D**ad pick up **M**other at the train station?
> I like staying with my grandmother.

The names of days, months, and holidays are capitalized, but the names of seasons are not.

> On **M**onday, **M**arch 12, Sasha will interview the mayor.
> Our family always has a picnic on **I**ndependence **D**ay.

The pronoun *I* is capitalized.

> Michael and **I** went to the video store.

···

Show What You Know

Circle the twenty-three letters that should be capitalized.

galileo was an Italian astronomer and physicist. he was born in Italy on february 15, 1564. in 1609 galileo built his first telescope. i heard about galileo when i went to a planetarium with my father. the guide also talked about the edwin p. hubble Space Telescope, which was released on sunday, april 15, 1990. he spoke of the mission that made repairs on the telescope in 1993. col. richard o. covey and dr. n. jan davis were part of the crew that repaired the telescope.

Score: _____   **Total Possible: 23**

2

Proofread

Here are some famous quotations. They are missing six capital letters.
Use the proper proofreading mark to show which letters should be capitalized.

Example: Eleanor Roosevelt said, "no one can make you feel inferior without your consent."

1. "and so, my fellow Americans," said John F. Kennedy, "ask not what your country can do

   for you; ask what you can do for your country."

2. Gertrude Stein said, "a rose is a rose is a rose is a rose."

3. "what's in a name?" asked Romeo. "that which we call a rose by any othe   me would

   smell as sweet."

4. "always do right," said Mark Twain. "This will gratify some people and astonish the rest."

5. "in spite of everything, I still believe," Anne Frank said, "that people

   are really good at heart."

Practice

Work with a partner. Think of three questions to ask
each other. Write your partner's answers as direct
quotations. Try writing one of the answers as a
divided quotation. When both of you are finished,
check each other's writing for correct capitalization.

Tips for Your Own Writing: Proofreading ....

The next time you write a story, make sure to write a conversation for two or more of your characters.
Capitalize the first word in each quotation and the first word in the second part of a divided quotation
only when it begins a new sentence.

What do sentences and quotations have in common? Their first words are always capped.

Capitalization: Friendly and Business Letters

 first words in certain parts of letters, such as greetings and closings, need capital le rs.

....**Did You Know?**............................

There   e two kinds of letters: friendly letters and business letters. Each kind o   tter has its own form, but both letters have a greeting and a closing   he first word in a greeting is capitalized. So are any names or titles us   in the greeting. Only the first word in a closing is capitalized.

Friendly Letter	Business Letter

Friendly Letter

1296 Meadow Drive
Glenview, IL 60025
August 17, 2000

Dear Ter...
I have bee   me for a week, but it seems much   ng   I really miss you and Rico. I had su   a g   d time staying at your ranch

You friend,

Carolina

Business Letter

1296 Meadow Drive
Glenview, IL 60025
December 2, 2000

Appleby, Incorporated
1348 Forest Avenue
Houston, TX 77069

Dear **S**ir or **M**adam:
I am returning the sweater you sent. I ordered a Large and received a Small. Please send me the correct size.

Sincerely yours,
Carolina Ramirez
Carolina Ramirez

....

how What ou Know

C cle each word that hould begin with a c ital letter.

1.   ear aunt katherine,

2.   ur patient cousin,

3.   pe to hear from you on,

4.   r mr. oglethorpe:

5.   cerely,

6. dea ustomer service department:

7. yours   ly,

Score: _____   **Total Possible: 14**

Proofread

Here are two short friendly letters. There are five missing capital letters in each. Use the proper proofreading mark to show which letters should be capitalized.

Example: My aunt kathy will arrive in may.

129 Wickam Way
Hillville, NJ 08505
April 28, 2000

dear uncle fred,

    mom told me that you fell down the

back steps and sprained your ankle. I'm

sending you several of my favorite books

to help pass the time.

       your nephew,

       Wilson

4490 Main Street
Weston, IA 50201
may 4, 2000

dear wilson,

    The books arrived, and i have already

read one. Thank you for thinking of me. A

sprained ankle is painful and boring!

       love,

       Uncle Fred

Practice

Think of a school or community problem. Write a letter to the editor of your local paper explaining the problem and your solutions to the problem. Write a draft of the body of your letter on the lines below. Then, using the business form, write the entire letter on a separate sheet of paper.

_____

_____

_____

_____

_____

_____

_____

Tips for Your Own Writing: Proofreading...

Look at a letter or note you have written recently. Check to see that you capitalized the appropriate words in the greeting and closing.

 A phone call is nice, but a letter is better!

6 Review: Capitalization

A. Use the proper proofreading mark to fix thirty missing capital letters.

last saturday, which was august 23, my brother bill married suzanne. it's about time, too, because everyone has been working on that wedding since valentine's day! my sister jenny was the maid of honor, and i was an usher. it was hot, crowded, and uncomfortable. when rev. benson finally introduced mr. and mrs. william j. krupski, i wanted to cheer. of course, mom was crying, but then so were dad, aunt shirley, uncle dave, and lots of other people. maybe they were just glad it was over, as i was!

Score: _____   Total Possible: 30

B. Use the proper proofreading mark to show fifteen words (names of places, buildings, groups, religions) that should begin with capital letters.

In northwest cambodia, not far from its border with thailand, lies the ruined city of angkor. From about 880 to about 1225, angkor was the capital of the mighty Khmer Empire. The city has several temple complexes, all larger than the egyptian pyramids, that were built to honor hindu gods. The greatest of these temples is angkor wat. Its vast stone walls are covered with scenes from hindu mythology. Angkor was abandoned about 1434, and the capital was moved to phnom penh. Rediscovered by french missionaries in the 1860s and now regarded as one of southeast asia's great masterpieces, Angkor has begun to attract many tourists from the west.

Score: _____   Total Possible: 15

C. Write the titles from the title and paragraph below in the blanks on the following page, adding capital letters where they are needed. If the title is in italics, also underline it.

that versatile writer: edgar allan poe

Edgar Allan Poe wrote his first book *tamerlane and other poems* in 1827 when he was 18. He soon began writing fiction. Five of his stories were published in a newspaper, the *philadelphia saturday courier*, and a sixth story won a $50 prize. Poe then became editor of a magazine, the *southern literary messenger*. His story "the murders in the rue morgue" is considered to be the first classic detective story. Some of his poems, such as "the raven," are still well-known today.

1. _____ 4. _____

2. _____ 5. _____

3. _____ 6. _____

Score: _____ Total Possible: 6

D. **Use the proper proofreading mark to add five capital letters where needed.**

"senator Brock," the reporter asked, "do you know Hiram M. Douglas?"

"no, I do not," said Senator Brock. "the name is unknown to me."

"but look at this picture," insisted the reporter. "isn't that you and Douglas?"

Score: _____ Total Possible: 5

E. **Use the proper proofreading mark under five lowercase letters that should be capitalized.**

1422 Bristol Road
Columbus, OH 43221
may 22, 2000

dear kaitlin,

thank you for the birthday present. It was very clever of you to remember how

much I liked Tina Weems's CD *Sweet Weems* and to give me a copy of my own. Isn't

Tina supposed to have a new CD next month?

your friend,

Tyesha

Score: _____ Total Possible: 5

REVIEW SCORE: _____ REVIEW TOTAL: 61

7 Punctuation: Sentences, Abbreviations, and Initials

✎ *Periods can be used to end a sentence, but they also let you know that a word is an abbreviation. That little dot is a valuable mark.*

............................Did You Know?...........................

A period is used at the end of a sentence that makes a statement.

> Football is a popular sport.

A period is used after abbreviations for titles, the months of the year, and the days of the week.

Doctor—Dr.	Mister—Mr.	Senator—Sen.
October—Oct.	January—Jan.	December—Dec.
Friday—Fri.	Wednesday—Wed.	Monday—Mon.

A period is used after initials in names.

> Susan Brownell Anthony—Susan **B.** Anthony
> Booker Taliaferro Washington—Booker **T.** Washington

Show What You Know

Read the paragraph below. First, add periods at ends of sentences where needed. Then, change each bold word to an initial or abbreviation by adding a period and drawing a line through the unnecessary letters. Circle each period.

Early on **Saturday**, the first of **November**, Joseph **Andrew** Simon got into his car. Mr. Simon is a teacher at Lyndon **Baines** Johnson High School. Every **Monday** and **Wednesday** in **September** and **October**, he taught exercise classes for some heart patients of Dr. **Pablo** Gonzalez These classes were held at Dwight **David** Eisenhower Elementary School The classes were so popular that other programs hired him. Every **Tuesday** and **Thursday** morning, he worked at Gerald **Rudolph** Ford University **Professor** Althea **Jane** Perkins sponsored the program. **Senator** Gutierrez and **Reverend** Tanaka participated in that class Now each Saturday in November and **December**, Mr. Simon will be coaching a wheelchair basketball team in the James **Francis** Thorpe fieldhouse.

Score: _____   **Total Possible: 23**

Proofread

Read these notes for a report. Use proper proofreading marks to add nine missing periods.

Example: Dr Bashir

    Margaret H Thatcher was born on Oct. 13, 1925 Mr and Mrs Alfred Roberts were her parents. The family lived in Grantham, Lincolnshire, England. After graduating, Margaret became a tax attorney and eventually was elected to Parliament in 1959 Becoming a member of Parliament is similar to being a senator in the United States government. Margaret Thatcher became the first woman leader of Britain's Conservative Party on Feb 11, 1975 Four years later on May 3, 1979, she was elected Prime Minister She resigned that post in Nov of 1990.

Practice

Write notes to summarize the events of the school week. Write your notes in complete sentences, and use abbreviations when possible.

1. _____

   _____

2. _____

   _____

3. _____

4. _____

5. _____

Tips for Your Own Writing: Proofreading..

Look for lists, notes, and other informal writing you have done. Check your writing to make sure you put a period at the end of sentences that are statements, and after initials, abbreviations, and each title.

Remember . . . periods put an end to statements and abbreviations.

8 Punctuation: Other Abbreviations

Don't be fooled—there are some abbreviations that do not use periods!

Did You Know?

Two-letter postal abbreviations for state names do not have periods. See page 160 for a complete list.

Tennessee—TN   California—CA
Idaho—ID   New York—NY

Abbreviations for metric measurements do not have periods.

meter—m   kilogram—kg   milliliter—mL
liter—L   gram—g   kilometer—km

Initials for the names of organizations or companies do not use periods.

American Broadcasting Companies—ABC
Boy Scouts of America—BSA

Some terms that are made up of more than one word are known by their initials. These do not use periods.

videocassette recorder—VCR
gross national product—GNP

Show What You Know

Write the abbreviations or initials for the following items.

1. Indiana _____

2. milligram _____

3. Texas _____

4. centimeter _____

5. Illinois _____

6. Nevada _____

7. Maine _____

8. Washington _____

9. kiloliter _____

10. Florida _____

11. National Basketball Association _____

12. recreational vehicle _____

13. American Heart Association _____

14. World Health Organization _____

15. Eastern Standard Time _____

16. Environmental Protection Agency _____

17. decimeter _____

18. most valuable player _____

19. North Dakota _____

20. Unidentified Flying Object _____

Score: _____   Total Possible: 20

Proofread

Proofread this part of a report and change the bold words to abbreviations. Write the abbreviations on the lines below the report.

Hurricanes sweep the Gulf of Mexico during the summer months. The whirling storms can measure 200 to 300 **miles** (320 to 480 **kilometers**) in diameter. The eye of a hurricane travels at a speed of 10 to 15 **miles per hour,** or 16 to 24 kilometers per hour. The cloud forms may rise 10,000 **feet** (3048 **meters**) high and cover thousands of miles. One of the costliest hurricanes to strike the United States was Hurricane Andrew, which hit the Bahamas and headed **northwest** to **Florida** and **Louisiana** in 1992.

1. _____

2. _____

3. _____

4. _____

5. _____

6. _____

7. _____

8. _____

Practice

Find out about a storm in your state or imagine one that could hit. Write some notes using abbreviations. Your notes should be in complete sentences.

_____

_____

_____

_____

_____

_____

Tips for Your Own Writing: Proofreading..................................

Look at some of your math papers or science reports to find examples of measurements. Check to see that you wrote the metric and customary measurement abbreviations correctly.

 *A*bbreviations save time and space when you are taking notes or making lists.

9 Punctuation: End Marks

"What does this say this is confusing" Can you read those sentences? Punctuation marks will make them clear! "What does this say? This is confusing."

Did You Know?

A period is used at the end of a sentence that makes a statement.

> Machines help us with many daily tasks**.**

A period is used at the end of a sentence that gives an order or makes a request.

> Turn on the dishwasher**.**

A question mark is used at the end of a sentence that asks a question.

> How many machines do you use each day**?**

An exclamation point is used at the end of a statement, order, or request that expresses strong feeling.

> That machine is awesome**!**
> Pull that plug right now**!**

Show What You Know

Put the correct punctuation mark at the end of each sentence. Circle any periods you add so they will be easier to see.

Do you think robots will replace the workforce I doubt it However, many of tomorrow's jobs will be performed by robots Think about the advantages this will bring for humans They can do work that is dangerous for people to do Noise, heat, smoke, and dust do not bother them Neither does the freezing cold of outer space A built-in computer controls a robot's actions so it can be programmed to do many difficult jobs

The word *robot* comes from the Czech word *robota*, which means "drudgery" What does *drudgery* mean It's work that is repetitive and tiresome Robots don't care what the task is They can work twenty-four hours a day at a steady pace Best of all, they never make mistakes How super Robots never get bored and they never complain They are truly special

Score: _____   **Total Possible: 17**

Proofread

Use proofreading marks to add twelve end punctuation marks where they are needed.

Example: I love to swim⊙

Hiking is one of the most enjoyable forms of exercise. Walking is a form of hiking Almost anyone can do it. All you really need is comfortable clothing and very comfortable walking shoes Shoes are probably the most important hiking tool. You will be on your feet a lot, so take care of them Get properly fitting shoes to avoid blisters and sore feet It's also wise to check the weather report before you start. You can then select the correct type of clothing

Find a special place to walk It can be on a sidewalk in a park, a trail in the forest, or a path in the country What can be better than walking along in a wooded area Nothing on earth As you walk, the sights and sounds of nature are all around you You hear the leaves rustling. Are you listening to the birds What beautiful sounds

Practice

There are many kinds of exercise. What is your favorite? Write a paragraph about your favorite exercise that will convince your friends it is a great activity.

_____

_____

_____

_____

_____

_____

_____

Tips for Your Own Writing: Proofreading..................................

Select a story you have recently written. Check to see if you put periods after sentences that are statements, orders, or requests, question marks after questions, and exclamation points after sentences that express strong feelings.

✐ *Punctuation is the key to others understanding what you write. Use the right marks when you write!*

10 Punctuation: Sentences

Sentences that run into each other need end punctuation. Use end punctuation marks to separate them.

·····································**Did You Know?**·····································

Two or more sentences written as though they were one sentence are hard to read. Correct use of end punctuation and capital letters will help you write better sentences.

> **Incorrect punctuation:** Sundials, water clocks, and hourglasses were the earliest timekeepers they were made from natural materials in the A.D. 1000s, mechanical clocks were invented in China.

> **Correct punctuation:** Sundials, water clocks, and hourglasses were the earliest timekeepers. They were made from natural materials. In the A.D. 1000s, mechanical clocks were invented in China.

A comma cannot be used as an end mark. Two sentences separated by only a comma are incorrectly punctuated.

> **Incorrect punctuation:** Sundials tell time by measuring the angle of the shadow cast by the sun, hourglasses do not.

> **Correct punctuation:** Sundials tell time by measuring the angle of the shadow cast by the sun. Hourglasses do not.

Show What You Know

Add periods where they are needed to correct the punctuation in this paragraph. Then circle the words that should be capitalized.

Early European mechanical clocks were huge the gears of the mechanical clocks often

occupied whole rooms they had no dials or hands but marked the time by ringing a bell these

clocks, like other early clocks, were inaccurate by 1400, the mechanical timekeeper had

become a part of everyday life almost every town had an enormous "town clock."

Score: _____   Total Possible: 10

Proofread

The paragraph below has four places where the punctuation is incorrect. Correct the sentences by using proper proofreading marks to add four end punctuation marks and four capital letters.

Example: Seals are interesting animals they are found in many parts of the world.

Harbor seals spend most of their time on floating ice chunks or land bearded seals enjoy spending their time in the same way. Harbor seals weigh between 100 and 150 pounds. They are usually about five feet in length. The weight of the larger bearded seals can be up to 1,500 pounds they can grow to be twelve feet long. Harbor seals like to play in groups bearded seals are happy spending time alone. Seals have generally poor hearing, but their sight is good. Bearded seals have big, brushlike whiskers harbor seals have small, delicate ones.

Practice

Choose a pair of the animals in the picture and write a paragraph comparing them. How are they alike? How are they different? When you are finished, reread your paragraph to check for sentences that are missing end marks.

_____

_____

_____

_____

_____

_____

_____

_____

_____

Tips for Your Own Writing: Proofreading...

The next time you write a report, check for sentences that need end marks. Read the sentences aloud to listen for mistakes in end punctuation.

Punctuation marks will help mark "the end" of sentences.

11 Punctuation: Sentence Fragments

"When I got on the bus." Is this a sentence? Add the missing parts to make a complete sentence.

Did You Know?

A sentence fragment is a group of words that is not a sentence. A *fragment* is a part of a sentence.

> **Fragment:** Until it got dark.
> **Sentence:** We played baseball until it got dark.
>
> **Fragment:** After we ate dinner.
> **Sentence:** After we ate dinner, we did our homework.

Show What You Know

Rewrite the paragraph to eliminate the sentence fragments. You can do this by adding the fragment to the beginning or end of the sentence it should be part of.

Itaipú, the most powerful electricity-producing dam in the world, is in Brazil. Paraguay and Brazil built the dam on the Paraná River. Which is in an area of dense tropical vegetation. The dam is 633 feet high and 5 1/2 miles long. After the dam was completed in 1991. The total cost of building it was determined to be $18 billion. The dam contains enough building materials to build a city for four million people. Because the water running over the dam sounds like music. It is called Itaipú, which means "singing dam" in Portuguese.

_____

_____

_____

_____

_____

_____

Score: _____   **Total Possible: 3**

Proofread

Eliminate the three sentence fragments by adding the fragments to the beginning or end of a sentence.

George Washington Carver helped save farm industry in the South by showing farmers how to rotate crops. Which means to plant different crops from year to year. Through his bulletins and speeches. Carver taught farmers many things. He spent many years researching peanuts. Which was one of his great achievements.

1. _____

_____

2. _____

_____

3. _____

_____

Practice

Write a paragraph that tells what you believe to be the most exciting summer Olympic sport to watch. Give reasons for your choice. Be sure to use complete sentences.

_____

_____

_____

_____

_____

_____

Tips for Your Own Writing: Proofreading..................................

Choose a favorite piece of your writing. Reading your work aloud can help you find sentence fragments. Some writers find it helps to "hear" problem sentence fragments if they read their papers "backwards," starting with the last sentence first.

 Remember to make sentences "whole"—no parts or fragments allowed.

23

Lesson 12 Review: Punctuation

A. Read these notes. Use the proper proofreading mark to add ten missing periods after sentences, abbreviations, and initials.

In an address to Congress in 1961, Pres. Kennedy called for a commitment to land a man on the moon before the end of the 1960s. *Apollo 8* was launched on Dec. 21, 1968. Astronauts James A. Lovell, William Anders, and Frank Borman were on board. The spacecraft reached the moon on Tues. the 24th and proceeded to make ten orbits around the moon. Splashdown occurred early on Fri. the 27th of Dec.

Score: _____   Total Possible: 10

B. Write an abbreviation for each bold term.

In math class today we used formulas to change measurement systems. We changed **miles** (_____) to **kilometers** (_____) and **feet** (_____) to **meters** (_____). Then we used
                          1   2   3   4
the map scale to measure the distance of the Oregon Trail from Independence, **Missouri** (_____), to Fort Walla Walla, **Washington** (_____). Finally, we calculated the
              5   6
travel time on the trail for a wagon and a **recreational vehicle** (_____). We discovered that
                                                                            7
the **miles per hour** (_____) were very different!
                    8

Score: _____   Total Possible: 8

C. Use the proper proofreading marks to add seven missing end punctuation marks to these directions.

Have you ever made homemade clay These directions will help you create a small quantity of clay. Take one cup of warm water, one cup of salt, and two cups of cooking flour Mix the ingredients together Squeeze the wet flour until it is smooth and does not stick to your fingers. It's ready for modeling You can create any type of sculpture you wish You may also want to add food coloring to various batches to make colorful figures of clay Have fun

Score: _____   Total Possible: 7

D. The paragraph below has three incorrect sentences. Correct the sentences using proper proofreading marks to add three end punctuation marks and three capital letters.

For many years, people in the United States used streetcars to travel in cities. At first, streetcars were called horsecars because they were pulled by horses. Later, streetcars were powered by steam in the 1800s, people began trying to use electric power, but making electricity was considered to be too expensive. In 1888 a machine was invented that made electricity inexpensively. In that same year, the first electric-powered streetcars were put into use they quickly replaced the steam-powered streetcar. With the invention of the gas engine, electric streetcars were soon replaced by buses and cars. By 1930 the streetcar had begun to disappear from city streets. Interest in streetcars revived in the 1970s streetcars use less energy per person and create less pollution than automobiles.

Score: _____   Total Possible: 6

E. Find and circle five sentence fragments. Then rewrite the paragraph by adding each fragment to the end of a sentence.

Garrett A. Morgan invented the gas mask. Morgan had to prove that his mask would work. Before people would use it. He showed a man going into a small tent. That was filled with smoke. The man stayed in the tent. For about twenty minutes. Next, the man went into a small room filled with poison gas. He stayed for fifteen minutes and was fine. When he came out. In 1916 Morgan used his gas mask to rescue more than twenty workers. Who were trapped in a smoke-filled tunnel in Cleveland.

_____

_____

_____

_____

_____

_____

Score: _____   Total Possible: 5

REVIEW SCORE: _____   REVIEW TOTAL: 36

13 Punctuation: Commas

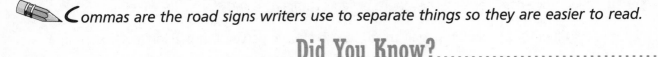

Commas are the road signs writers use to separate things so they are easier to read.

Did You Know?

Commas are used to separate three or more items in a series. Put a comma after each item except for the last one.

Rolls, bagels, scones, and muffins are displayed in the bakery.
Customers can see, smell, and admire the different kinds of bread.
I bought carrot muffins, rye rolls, blueberry scones, and onion bagels.

Commas are used after introductory words such as *yes*, *no*, and *well*.

Yes, that bakery makes the best sourdough bread in the city.
Well, you have to get there early before the bread is gone.

An appositive follows a noun and gives more information about the noun. In the examples below, the appositives are in bold type. Commas are used to set off appositives from the rest of a sentence.

Mr. Schultz, **the bakery owner,** is very proud of his breads.
My favorite is pumpernickel, **a sour rye bread**.

Commas are used in direct address. Commas separate the name of the person spoken to from the rest of the sentence.

Do you have any wheat bread, Mr. Schultz?
Jerry, I put a loaf aside just for you.
You know, Mr. Schultz, you are a wonderful man!

Show What You Know

Read the paragraph. Add fourteen commas where they are needed.

Dogs come in all sizes shapes and colors. The American Kennel Club the official dog breeding organization recognizes 130 breeds in seven categories. For example, sporting dogs include pointers setters and retrievers. Collies sheepdogs and corgis are considered herding dogs. Ben my boxer is classified as a working dog. But to me, Ben is a companion. When I say, "Ben come," he always comes. Well maybe he doesn't *always* come. But he certainly comes when I say, "Dinner Ben." Yes *dinner* is definitely a word he knows!

Score: _____   Total Possible: 14

Proofread

Add eleven commas to this conversation where they are needed. Use the proper proofreading mark to show where each comma should be placed.

Example: Well, are you ready to begin?

"Lionel, I've got the telescope, two blankets, and some hot chocolate. Let's go outside

and look at the moon, the stars, and the planets."

"Well, I don't know, Lucy. Will there be any snakes, spiders, or bats out there?"

"No, I don't think so, Lionel. Annie Callahan, my next-door neighbor goes out star-gazing

every night. So does Harry Thoreaux, your dentist. Last night he saw a meteor. Wouldn't you

like to see a meteor, Lionel?"

"Yes, Lucy I would. But only if I don't have to see any rats, roaches or worms!"

"Then I suggest you look up Lionel, rather than down!"

Practice

Write a paragraph in which you describe your favorite foods to a friend. In the first sentence, list at least three different foods. Then describe them. Use your friend's name in at least one sentence.

_____

_____

_____

_____

_____

_____

_____

Tips for Your Own Writing: Proofreading...

Choose a piece of your own writing and ask a partner to proofread it, checking for commas between items in a series and with introductory words, appositives, and direct address.

 Commas separate things to make your writing as clear as a bell.

14 Punctuation: Commas After Phrases and Clauses

Sentences are easier to read and understand when commas are used to set off phrases and clauses at the beginning of the sentences.

······························Did You Know?······························

A comma is used after a long prepositional phrase at the beginning of a sentence. A comma is not necessary if the prepositional phrase is very short. A prepositional phrase is a group of words that begins with a preposition such as *at, in, on,* and *of.*

> On a beautiful August morning, Mark went climbing.
> At noon he reached the mountain peak.
> In 1998 Mark climbed his highest peak.

A comma is used after a subordinate clause at the beginning of a sentence. A subordinate clause is a group of words that begins with a subordinate conjunction such as *after, although, before, if, unless, when,* and *while.* Even though the clause has a subject and a verb, it cannot stand alone as a sentence.

> After he got to the top, Mark sat down to rest.
> While he was resting, he admired the view.

Show What You Know

Add seven commas where they are needed in this paragraph.

After La Salle explored the area the French claimed the land in 1682 and called it Louisiana. After the French and Indian wars in the 1700s France had to give Louisiana to Spain. In 1800 Spain had to give Louisiana back to France. Although Napoleon I wanted an American empire he wanted money more. In 1803 he decided to sell Louisiana. For about $15 million the United States could buy the land. When President Thomas Jefferson heard about the offer he was delighted. Before Napoleon could change his mind Jefferson bought the land. With one bold, decisive stroke the United States doubled in size.

Score: _____   **Total Possible: 7**

28

Proofread

Read this paragraph and add four commas that are needed. Use the proper proofreading mark to show where each comma should be added.

Example: After grapes have been dried‸they're called raisins.

If you want something good to eat, have some raisins. For a long, long time I didn't like raisins. But one day there wasn't anything else to eat, so I popped a few raisins in my mouth. As I chewed I realized, hey, these are good! Now I eat them all the time. At lunch I have a box for dessert. After a long day at school I have a box as a snack. When I get the urge to munch I go for the raisins. Without a doubt, I am now a raisin raver.

Practice

Describe what is happening in these pictures. Write your description on the lines below. Try to begin some of your sentences with subordinate conjunctions or prepositions.

_____

_____

_____

_____

_____

_____

_____

_____

_____

Tips for Your Own Writing: Proofreading...

The next time you write a report, check to see if you used any long phrases or clauses to introduce sentences and used commas to set off those phrases and clauses from the rest of their sentences.

 _T_hink of commas as places to pause briefly.

15 Punctuation: Semicolons and Colons

Semicolons and colons look a lot alike. Semicolons separate sentences. Colons come before lists, after the greeting in a business letter, and in numbers used to tell time.

................................Did You Know?................................

A semicolon (;) can be used when combining two related sentences.

> I rushed to the shelf; the book was already gone.

A semicolon also can be placed before a conjunction such as *besides*, *however*, *nevertheless*, *moreover*, and *therefore*, when combining two related sentences. A comma should be placed after those conjunctions. When using a conjunction such as *and*, *but*, or *or*, place a comma, not a semicolon, before the conjunction.

> The book is very popular; **therefore,** it is hard to find.
> I rushed to the shelf, **but** the book was already gone.

A colon (:) is used before a list of items. Usually, the colon follows a noun or pronoun. Do not use a colon after a verb or a preposition that introduces a list.

> I looked for these books: a mystery, a biography, and an almanac.
> The library has books, magazines, CDs, and audiocassettes.

A colon is also used between the numbers for hours and minutes in time.

> The library opens at 9:00 A.M. and closes at 5:30 P.M.

A colon is used after the greeting in a business letter.

> Dear Ms. Sloan:

....

Show What You Know

Read the paragraph. Add semicolons and colons where they are needed.

At 900 P.M. I watched a program about Pompeii. Pompeii was a Roman city in southern Italy it was located near a volcano, Mt. Vesuvius. The people thought Vesuvius was extinct however, they were wrong. On August 24, A.D. 79, Vesuvius proved it was active it erupted suddenly and violently. Thick layers of ash and rock buried these towns Herculaneum, Stabiae, and Pompeii. In 1748 Pompeii was excavated. These public buildings were found in the city center temple, council chamber, assembly hall, courthouse, and market.

Score: _____   Total Possible: 6

Proofread

Two semicolons and three colons are missing in the paragraph below. Use proper proofreading marks to show where each semicolon or colon should be placed.

Example: Caroline's alarm didn't go off at 7ᐱ00 A.M.ᐱ it was the beginning of a bad day.

Caroline sat fuming on the school bus; it was stuck in traffic on the highway. She tried to stay calm however, she was afraid she would be late for school. The deadline to sign up for the ski trip was this morning at 915. It was now 8:45. Mentally, Caroline made a list of things she could do: cry, scream, walk, or laugh. She tried to breathe deeply she tried to focus on a happy thought. No happy thoughts came to mind; nevertheless, she did feel a little better. It was now 905. There was nothing she could do; all the spots for the ski trip would be filled by the time she got to school. Caroline wrote the following notes return new ski hat, take up bowling, and sign up for special school activities earlier next time!

Practice

Imagine that you are having a party. Using complete sentences, write an invitation in which you tell your guests the kind of party, the date, the time, the place, and any other information you think they should know. Use colons and semicolons.

_____

_____

_____

_____

_____

_____

_____

Tips for Your Own Writing: Revising..

As you write your next report, think about the structure of your sentences. Are there any related sentences that you could combine using either a semicolon, or a semicolon and a conjunction? Are there any lists that you could rewrite using a colon?

Despite its name, a semicolon is not just half a colon. It's half a colon plus a comma!

16 Review: Commas, Colons, Semicolons

A. **Add twelve commas that are needed in the paragraph below. Use the proper proofreading mark to show where each comma should be placed.**

Hey I'm home Mom! Wow, I'm out of breath! I ran all the way because I didn't want to miss *Beanie and Frank* my favorite TV show. Tonight Beanie is finally going to tell Frank, Chloe and Spike her big secret. Sure, I can set the table now. The show doesn't start for ten minutes. Mom, will you please get Joey Donna, and the dog out of here? No take the dog with you Joey! Donna that little whiner, really gets on my nerves. Okay, I'm finished. Mom if I can just watch this show the one I've been waiting to see, all by myself, I promise I'll wash dry, and put away the dishes after dinner without being asked. Thanks Mom.

Score: _____   **Total Possible: 12**

B. **Correct the punctuation by either making two separate sentences or combining them with a comma and a conjunction (and, but, or). Write the sentences on the lines.**

1. Other people may prefer roses or orchids I like sunflowers best.

   Other people may prefer roses or orchids, but I like sunflowers best.

2. Sunflowers turn their heads to face the sun they also look like little suns.

   Sunflowers turn their heads to face the sun and they also look like little suns

3. They have large heads of yellow flowers the heads contain many small black seeds.

   _____

4. Sunflowers grow in people's gardens they are grown as a crop.

   _____

5. The seeds are processed for vegetable oil they are used as bird food.

   _____

6. Birds may like to eat sunflower seeds so do people.

   _____

Score: _____   **Total Possible: 6**

C. Add two commas where needed in this paragraph. Use the proper proofreading mark to show where each comma should be added.

In the mid-nineteenth century, the main overland route to the Northwest was the Oregon Trail. From Independence, Missouri, people walked 2,000 miles to reach the Williamette Valley in Oregon. In 1836, a group of missionary families made the long trip on the trail. When people back East read the reports of the trip, many of them decided to go to Oregon, too. By 1846 more than 6,000 people had used the Oregon Trail. After gold was discovered in California in 1848 fewer people made the trek to Oregon. Soon the trail was all but forgotten.

Score: _____   Total Possible: 2

D. Add five commas where they are needed to make the sentences less confusing to read. Use the proper proofreading mark to show where each comma should be added.

When the storm hit, Maya was working at home. She waited patiently, for the storm would soon be over. Maya held her dog, and her cat hid under the bed. By the time the storm had finished, the power lines were down. Inside the house was dark but safe.

Score: _____   Total Possible: 5

E. Add either one semicolon or one colon to each sentence in the paragraph below. Use proper proofreading marks to show where they should be added.

Every day at 615 A.M., the alarm clock goes off and Jenny gets out of bed. She always does the same things wash face, brush teeth, get dressed, and eat breakfast. Jenny always eats a bowl of cornflakes she always drinks a glass of milk. Jenny laughs about her routine however, she has no intention of changing it.

Score: _____   Total Possible: 4

REVIEW SCORE: _____   REVIEW TOTAL: 29

17 Punctuation: Dialogue—Commas and End Marks

Commas and periods always go within closing quotation marks. No questions asked. Exclamation points and question marks are open to question, aren't they?

·······································Did You Know?·······························

Commas and periods are *always* placed inside closing quotation marks.

> "Until 1996**,**" the sports fan said, "the Los Angeles Lakers held the record for the most team wins in a single season**.**"

Question marks and exclamation points are placed inside the closing quotation marks if they are part of the quotation.

> Her friend asked, "How many games did the Lakers win in one season**?**"

Question marks and exclamation points are placed outside the closing quotation marks if they are *not* part of the quotation.

> How exciting to hear, "The Bulls broke the Lakers' record"**!**

Show What You Know

Add a total of twenty-nine quotation marks, commas, and end punctuation where they are needed in the sentences.

How excited Jan was when she heard the sportscaster say, Last night the Chicago Bulls

broke the team record for games won in a single season

The Bulls broke the record she shouted as she ran into my room.

I asked calmly, What record did they break

Jan asked How could you not know? Don't you pay attention to sports

No I replied. I don't pay much attention to sports

How could I have known that Jan was about to give me a crash course in sports trivia

when she said, Come over here and sit down.

The Chicago Bulls just won seventy games for this season Jan explained and that's the

most games ever won in a single season by an NBA team

Score: _____   **Total Possible: 29**

34

Proofread

Read this conversation between two sportscasters. Use proper proofreading marks to add eleven missing quotation marks, commas, and end punctuation marks.

Example: I told my family "There is absolutely no sport as exciting as basketball!"

Bart said Listen to the crowd shouting!" The Chicago Bulls had just won their seventy-second game of the 1995–1996 season. "Who would have believed that we would be sitting here tonight announcing that the Chicago Bulls have established a new record for the most games won in a single season

"Yes," said Bob. "it wasn't too long ago that people were asking whether the Bulls could break the record

Now that the Bulls have won their seventy-second game, said Bart people are asking me whether the Bulls' record can be broken"

Bob replied, "Only time will tell."

Practice

Think about an exciting sports event you have participated in or seen. Write a dialogue between you and a friend in which you talk about the event. Remember to start a new paragraph each time the speaker changes.

_____

_____

_____

_____

_____

_____

Tips for Your Own Writing: Proofreading..

The next time you write a story, include some dialogue. Make sure you place all periods and commas within closing quotation marks, and question marks and exclamation points outside quotation marks in quoted material.

In or out—"Watch your quotation marks and end punctuation!"

18 Punctuation: Direct and Indirect Quotations

✏️ *Adam said, "Take it directly from me. This is a direct quotation." He then added that an indirect quotation restates something that was said.*

....**Did You Know?**..

A direct quotation is the exact words someone said or wrote. A direct quotation is enclosed within quotation marks.

> Abraham Lincoln said, **"A house divided against itself cannot stand."**

An indirect quotation is a restatement or rephrasing of something said or written. An indirect quotation is *not* enclosed in quotation marks.

> Abraham Lincoln said that **a house in which there is no unity cannot withstand pressure from outside forces.**

An indirect quotation is often introduced by the word *that*, and a comma is not used to separate the speaker's tag from the indirect quotation.

> Abraham Lincoln said **that** a house in which there is no unity cannot withstand pressure from outside forces.

Show What You Know

Decide whether each sentence includes a direct or an indirect quotation. If a sentence includes a direct quotation, add quotation marks where they are needed. If a sentence is an indirect quotation, write *indirect* on the line.

1. In one speech, Abraham Lincoln commented, The ballot is stronger than the bullet._____

2. Lincoln said in a campaign speech that no one would ever consider him a person who

would become a President._____

3. What is conservatism? is a question Lincoln once asked._____

4. Discouraged by news during the Civil War, Lincoln noted in 1861, If McClellan is not using

the army, I should like to borrow it for a while._____

5. Lincoln stated that persons must stand firm in their important basic beliefs._____

6. In a letter to the editor, Lincoln noted that he supported giving the privileges of government to all

those who helped bear the burdens of being involved in government._____

Score: _____ **Total Possible: 9**

Proofread

Read the article about Lincoln. It contains eight errors in punctuation involving direct and indirect quotations. Use proper proofreading marks to correct the errors.

Example: Mrs. Rainbucket said, "How about grabbing an umbrella? Mr. Hailstorm said that,

"We could expect wet weather."

Abraham Lincoln attended school less than a year but actually wrote his own math book. He said, There were some schools, so called, but no qualification was ever required of a teacher, beyond readin', writin', and cipherin', to the Rule of Three.

One book that made a lasting impression on Abe was *Life of Washington.* Of this book he said, I recollect thinking then, boy even though I was, that there must have been something more than common that those men struggled for.

Lincoln became a lawyer simply by reading law books to familiarize himself with the law. He said that, "If someone is resolutely determined to make a lawyer of himself, the thing is more than half done already."

Practice

Imagine that you are a reporter who interviewed Abraham Lincoln during the Civil War. Write an article, using direct and indirect quotations.

_____

_____

_____

_____

_____

_____

_____

_____

Tips for Your Own Writing: Proofreading..

See if you can find a piece of your own writing that includes direct and indirect quotations. Make sure the speaker's tags are separated from direct quotations with commas, both opening and closing quotation marks are used, quotation marks with indirect quotations were avoided, and indirect quotations were introduced by the word *that*.

✏️ *K*nowing who said what and what was said puts a reader in the know!

19 Punctuation: Friendly and Business Letters

Are you sending a friendly or a business letter? The only major differences are that business letters have an inside address, and the greeting is followed by a colon.

Did You Know?

A friendly letter and a business letter both have distinct parts. The only difference in punctuation is following the greeting. A comma is used in a friendly letter and a colon in a business letter.

Friendly Letter

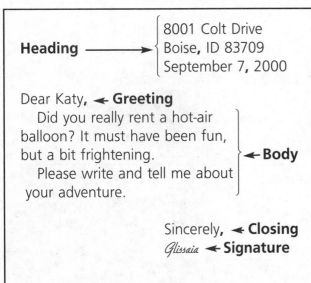

Heading →
8001 Colt Drive
Boise, ID 83709
September 7, 2000

Dear Katy, ◄ **Greeting**
   Did you really rent a hot-air balloon? It must have been fun, but a bit frightening.
   Please write and tell me about your adventure. ◄ **Body**

Sincerely, ◄ **Closing**
Glissaia ◄ **Signature**

Business Letter

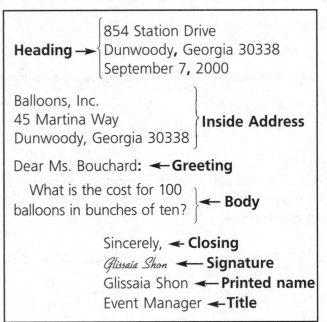

Heading →
854 Station Drive
Dunwoody, Georgia 30338
September 7, 2000

Balloons, Inc.
45 Martina Way
Dunwoody, Georgia 30338 } **Inside Address**

Dear Ms. Bouchard: ◄ **Greeting**
   What is the cost for 100 balloons in bunches of ten? ◄ **Body**

Sincerely, ◄ **Closing**
Glissaia Shon ◄ **Signature**
Glissaia Shon ◄ **Printed name**
Event Manager ◄ **Title**

Show What You Know

Add punctuation where it is needed in this friendly letter to correct the four errors.

248 Sexton Drive
Mettawa Illinois 60045
September 2 2000

Dear Karin
   We made a hot-air balloon for our school play by attaching a plastic cloth to a cardboard box, and filling the cloth with helium-filled balloons. It looked great!
   Your friend
   Madrena

Score: _____   Total Possible: 4

Proofread

Correct the punctuation in this business letter. Use proper proofreading marks to correct the five errors.

Example: Sea Isle City, FL 34746

513 Elm Wood Place
Kansas City, Missouri, 64112
August 23 2000

Country Music Association
One Music Circle South
Nashville Tennessee 37203

Dear Music Director

Our band, Country Nights, has played together for more than eight years. We have recently written and performed a new song that we think you will like. The song "Days into Nights" is recorded on the enclosed tape. Please let us know if you are interested in this song and others we have written.

Sincerely

Mitch Fellfield

Mitch Fellfield
Manager, Country Nights Band

Practice

Think about a musical group that you would like to see perform. Write the body of a business letter to the group asking if they will be performing somewhere near you. Ask about prices, dates, and locations of the upcoming performances. On another sheet of paper, write your letter adding all the necessary parts.

_____

_____

_____

_____

Tips for Your Own Writing: Proofreading.....................................

Choose a letter you have recently written. Check the letter to make sure it has the correct parts and is correctly punctuated.

 Greetings to friends, use a comma in a letter. Greetings in business letters: use a colon.

Lesson
20 Review: Punctuation

A. Use proper proofreading marks to add commas and quotation marks to each sentence. You will need to make sixteen corrections.

1. Homer wrote "Your heart is always harder than a stone.

2. Absence," Sextus Propertius wrote, makes the heart grow fonder.

3. In *Othello,* Shakespeare wrote My heart is turned to stone.

4. And what my heart taught me wrote poet Robert Browning I taught the world.

5. But it is wisdom to believe the heart, wrote George Santayana in one of his poems.

Score: _____   Total Possible: 16

B. Read the conversation below. Use proper proofreading marks to add end punctuation and quotation marks where they are needed. You will need to make nineteen corrections.

How did Vice-President Harry Truman feel when he heard Mrs. Franklin D. Roosevelt say,

Harry, the President is dead

He gave a clue, when he said to the press, I felt like the moon, the stars, and all the

planets had fallen on me

Harry Truman, our teacher said, took over the presidency during World War II after

President Roosevelt died from a stroke

She then asked us, How did Truman indicate that he knew the job of being President

would be difficult

His comments to the press, Mai answered, showed that it would be difficult to replace

Roosevelt

Score: _____   Total Possible: 19

C. Use proper proofreading marks to add quotation marks to all direct quotations below. You will need to make sixteen corrections.

1. My younger brother asked, How many planets are there?

2. I told him that there were nine planets, and Earth was one of them.

3. Then he asked me if Earth was the largest planet.

4. No, I told him, Jupiter is the largest planet, and Earth is very small in comparison.

5. He continued to question me, asking, Is Earth the smallest planet?

6. I explained that Pluto was the smallest planet.

7. But Earth is the best planet, he said.

8. Yes, it is, I agreed, because only on Earth can plants and animals live.

9. Then he told me that Earth was the best planet because I lived here.

10. I laughed and said, No, Earth is the best because we both live here.

Score: _____   Total Possible: 16

D. Use proper proofreading marks to correct the nine errors in the paragraph below. Be sure to underline the names of books, plays, movies, newspapers, or magazines. Enclose the names of poems, articles, stories, or songs in quotation marks.

My partners and I are preparing a presentation about the Mississippi River. Jessica is reading a passage from Mark Twain's book Life on the Mississippi. Matt and Carlos are singing the song Ol' Man River from the play Show Boat. Sonia is reading part of the article The Great Flood of 1993 that appeared in the October 1993 issue of National Geographic World. I am providing background information and closing the presentation with a poem that my partners and I wrote. It is called The River of History.

Score: _____   Total Possible: 9

REVIEW SCORE: _____   REVIEW TOTAL: 60

21 Usage: Verbs—Froze, Shook, Rang

Verbs, or action words, come in different forms. Which form do you use?

....Did You Know?..

A verb is an action or being word in a sentence. It tells what happens or what is. The form that you use depends upon the action that is being described. For example, the past form of a verb describes a past action. It usually consists of one word. The past participle form consists of the past form that is used with a helping verb such as *have, has, had, was,* or *were.*

Look at the present, past, and past participle forms of each of the troublesome verbs below. Then read the sentences that follow. They show correct usage for each form of these verbs.

Present	Past	Past Participle
Today they **freeze**.	Yesterday they **froze**.	They **have frozen**.
Today they **shake**.	Yesterday they **shook**.	They **have shaken**.
Today they **ring**.	Yesterday they **rang**.	They **have rung**.

We **froze** peach ice cream on the Fourth of July.
Dad **had frozen** the hamburger meat that he cooked on the grill.

We **shook** the whole way home after seeing the action movie.
The city residents **had been shaken** by the disasters that occurred.

Tina **rang** the dinner bell for the members of the camp.
She **has rung** that bell every evening for twenty years.

....

Show What You Know

Underline the correct form of each verb in parentheses.

Carlos was worried. He was sure he had (froze, frozen) the ice cream dessert long
₁
enough. But would it be ready for the club members thirty minutes from now? Carlos took the

pan out of the freezer and (shook, shaken) it lightly. Well, no ripples disturbed the surface—a
₂
good sign! Just then the phone (rang, rung): Dana was sick and couldn't come. After the
₃
phone had (rang, rung) four more times, the meeting was off. Too many members were sick
₄
or busy. "I (froze, frozen) that dessert for nothing," said Carlos. "But this has not
₅
(shook, shaken) my confidence. I know I made a tasty treat!"
₆

Score: _____   Total Possible: 6

Proofread

The following TV editorial uses the verb pairs *froze/frozen*, *shook/shaken*, and *rang/rung*. Each verb form is used incorrectly once. Using the proper proofreading marks, delete each incorrect word and write the correction above it.

shaken
Example: The people were ~~shook~~ by the accident.

The people of this county have froze through one of our worst winters, and earthquakes

have shook our homes. We cannot blame nature on politicians. But we can blame them for

failing us. In a recent session, the state legislature frozen funds for earthquake relief. This act

shaken our faith in the government.

Just one week ago, we rung in a new year. Let us resolve to shake up the government.

Politicians, take notice: we have rang the alarm!

Practice

You may notice that the verbs in this lesson describe sensory actions. Write a strong sensory sentence for each verb in each pair. Use the same topic within each pair, but vary the sentences enough to make them interesting.

froze/frozen

_____

_____

_____

shook/shaken

_____

_____

_____

rang/rung

_____

_____

_____

Tips for Your Own Writing: Proofreading..

Choose a piece of your own writing. See whether you find any of the three verb pairs from this lesson and if you used the correct form of each verb.

Froze, shook, *and* rang *can stand by themselves, but* frozen, shaken, *and* rung *need a little help.*

22 Usage: Verbs—Swam, Tore, Took

*S*ome verbs don't conform to the patterns we expect. *Swam, swum? Tore, torn? Took, taken? How do you know which is right?*

......................................**Did You Know?**..................................

The past form of a verb describes a past action. It usually consists of one word. The past participle form consists of the past form that is used with a helping verb such as *have, has, had, was,* or *were.*

Look at the present, past, and past participle forms of each of the troublesome verbs below. Then read the sentences that follow. They show correct usage for each form of these verbs.

Present	Past	Past Participle
Today they **swim**.	Yesterday they **swam**.	They **have swum**.
Today they **tear**.	Yesterday they **tore**.	They **have torn**.
Today they **take**.	Yesterday they **took**.	They **have taken**.

The bluefish **swam** together in a vast school off the coast.
They **have swum** along this coast for hundreds of years.

"You **tore** the jacket!" gasped the actress.
The curtain **was torn** from the stage in the scuffle that followed.

"I think you **took** more than your share," complained the hungry camper.
But she **had taken** exactly what was her due.

....

Show What You Know

Write the word that best completes each sentence.

The bluefin tuna ___*tore*___ at its unfortunate prey. Then it ___*swam*___ swiftly toward
　　　　　　　1 (tore, torn)　　　　　　　　　　　　　　　　　**2** (swam, swum)

another victim. That helpless fish had ___*torn*___ one of its fins badly. A sea bass had
　　　　　　　　　　　　　　　3 (tore, torn)

___*taken*___ a large shrimp for its dinner. The shrimp had ___*swum*___ by lazily and carelessly.
4 (took, taken)　　　　　　　　　　　　　　　　**5** (swam, swum)

The hunter of the sea was no longer hungry, so it ___*took*___ no more victims.
　　　　　　　　　　　　　　　　　　　　　6 (took, taken)

Score: _____　　　　**Total Possible: 6**

44

Proofread

The following radio script uses the verb pairs *swam/swum*, *tore/torn*, and *took/taken*. Using the proper proofreading marks, delete four incorrect words and write the correction above each one.

Example: We ~~swum~~ ^swam^ for an hour.

NARRATOR: Here comes our hero, Pam Pekinese. Pam has swum across the lagoon in

record time. (*Sound effect for swimming.*)

PAM: I have swam my last mission! It's true that I'm the world's greatest swimming

Pekinese, but I have took all I can take! See? Those playful dolphins ~~torn~~ ^tore^ two

of my favorite hair ribbons. Yap, yip.

MEL MYNAH: You didn't expect any dolphins you swam by to pass up a chance to tease

you? They did the same thing when you swum by them last week.

NARRATOR: Tune in next week for "Strange Animals Do Strange Things."

Practice

Write a brief description of a giant squid attacking a boat at sea. Use all the verb pairs presented in this lesson. Choose other words carefully to give the story a strong sense of action.

_____

_____

_____

_____

_____

_____

_____

_____

Tips for Your Own Writing: Proofreading.............................

Choose a sample of your own writing. Look for *took/taken*, *swam/swum*, and *tore/torn*. Check to see that you used a helping verb with *taken*, *swum*, and *torn*.

If you swam through this lesson without hitting a snag, you have swum well!

Lesson
23 Usage: Verbs—Wrote, Stole, Began

Troublesome verbs refuse to conform. You have to learn them one by one—or two by two!

················· **Did You Know?** ·················

The past form of a verb describes a past action. It usually consists of one word. The <u>past participle</u> form consists of the past form that is used with a helping verb such as *have, has, had, was,* or *were.*

Look at the present, past, and past participle forms of each of the troublesome verbs below. Then read the sentences that follow. They show correct usage for each form of these verbs.

Present	Past	Past Participle
Today they **write**.	Yesterday they **wrote**.	They **have written**.
Today they **steal**.	Yesterday they **stole**.	They **have stolen**.
Today they **begin**.	Yesterday they **began**.	They **have begun**.

"Where is the poem that I **wrote?**" bellowed Milton.
The weary poet **had written** many stanzas last night.

Someone **stole** Hannah's gym shoes.
My favorite sneakers **were stolen** from the gym, also.

The mourning dove **began** its sorrowful song.
The birds **had begun** their chorus at 4:30 in the morning!

Show What You Know

Read the paragraph. Underline the correct form of each verb in parentheses.

In an ancient land called Sumer, scholars (wrote, written) on clay tablets with a stylus. The

¹

stylus was a tool that made wedge-shaped marks in wet clay. Young students (began, begun)

²

their education by learning to write with this tool. Why did the Sumerians develop this type of

writing? One reason was that they had (began, begun) to record laws. Writing down a code of

³

laws allows a society to apply laws equally. For example, Sumerian judges could punish any

powerful person who (stole, stolen) goods the same as anyone else who had (stole, stolen).

⁴ ⁵

Soon, people found easier ways to write. Keepers of records have not (wrote, written) on clay

⁶

tablets for centuries!

Score: _____   **Total Possible: 6**

46

Proofread

The following interview uses the verb pairs *wrote/written*, *stole/stolen*, and *began/begun*. Each verb form is used incorrectly once. Using the proper proofreading mark, delete each incorrect word and write the correction above it.

Example: We ~~begun~~ began our day early.

INTERVIEWER: Tell us what you have ~~wrote~~ written lately, Pete.

PETE PORTER: Well, Zara, I have been writing an epic poem about the dawn of the computer

age. Some critics might claim that I ~~stolen~~ stole the idea from Beryl Brinkley, but

that's not true.

INTERVIEWER: Critic Natalie Naster claimed that you had stole the rhymes. But enough of

that. You ~~written~~ wrote ten short poems last year, didn't you?

PETE PORTER: Right. But now I have began to create epic poetry!

INTERVIEWER: Fascinating. When you begun your career, we had no idea you'd write epic

poetry. We look forward to your new poem.

Practice

Imagine the dispute between poets Pete Porter and Beryl Brinkley. Write a short letter that one of these poets might write to the other one. Include the verbs presented in this lesson.

_____

_____

_____

_____

_____

_____

_____

Tips for Your Own Writing: Proofreading..

Choose a story you have written. See whether you find any of the three verb pairs from this lesson. Make sure you used a helping verb when necessary.

*"**W**rote/written, stole/stolen, began/begun—*
Learning verbs in pairs can be lots of fun!"

24 Usage: Verbs—Blew, Sank, Fell

✎ *Studying past forms of verbs in pairs gives us clues to solving verb mysteries. Elementary, my dear Watson!*

·····························Did You Know?·····························

The <u>past form</u> of a verb describes a past action. It usually consists of one word. The <u>past participle</u> form consists of the past form that is used with a helping verb such as *have, has, had, was,* or *were*.

Look at the present, past, and past participle forms of each of the troublesome verbs below. Then read the sentences that follow. They show correct usage for each form of these verbs.

Present	Past	Past Participle
Today they **blow**.	Yesterday they **blew**.	They **have blown**.
Today they **sink**.	Yesterday they **sank**.	They **have sunk**.
Today they **fall**.	Yesterday they **fell**.	They **have fallen**.

The wind **blew,** slapping rain across the deck.
Fiercer gales **had blown** before.

One storm last fall **sank** a freighter ten miles off the coast.
But no ship of mine **has** ever **sunk.**

In a shocking crash, the main mast **fell** to the deck!
It **had fallen** so suddenly, no one could sound a warning.

Show What You Know

In each pair of sentences, draw a line to match each sentence with the verb form that it should use.

The BBW Story (Big Bad Wolf)

1. The BBW had a reputation to keep up: he ____ houses down.   blown
   This wouldn't be the first straw hut he had ____ away.   blew

2. But when the pigs heard him, their hearts had ____ to their toes.   sank
   Before hiding, they ____ their valuables into the well.   sunk

3. What was the outcome? The house had ____—no big deal.   fallen
   "We really ____ for that huff-and-puff story," said Pig Junior.   fell

Score: _____   Total Possible: 6

Proofread

The following is an imaginary diary entry by a sailor in the 1700s. The writer used the verb pairs *blew/blown, sank/sunk,* and *fell/fallen* incorrectly six times. Using the proper proofreading mark, delete each incorrect word and write the correction above it.

Example: The sun ~~sunk~~ below the horizon.

> sank

At about 9:00 A.M., a gust of wind blown suddenly, shaking the ship to its keel. Just then

the second mate fell to the deck. Others had fell, too, so great was the jolt. The tempest blew,

and then it had blew some more. Another dreadful gust hit. "Have we sank for good?" cried

the first mate. "The enemy never sunk this scow," shouted Captain Cruz, "nor will Mother

Nature now!" When the wind had fell, we knew that the ship had not sunk.

Practice

Imagine that you are at sea on a boat like the one in the picture. Suddenly, an intense storm blows up. Describe the experience, using strong action verbs and vivid descriptive words. Also, use the three pairs of verbs presented in this lesson.

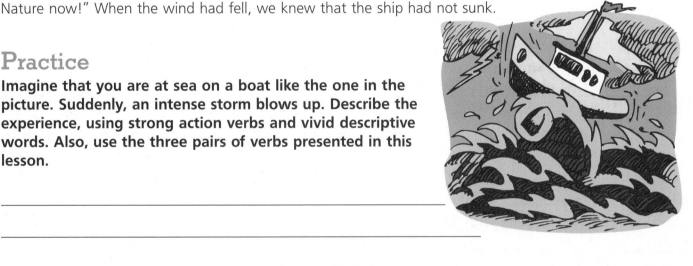

_____

_____

_____

_____

_____

_____

_____

_____

_____

_____

Tips for Your Own Writing: Proofreading......................................

Review a report you have written. Look for the words *blew/blown, sank/sunk,* and *fell/fallen.* Check the sentences to see that you have used a helping verb with *blown, sunk,* and *fallen.*

You neither sank nor fell in this lesson, nor have you sunk or fallen! If you blew your own horn, then you have blown it for good reason.

49

25 Usage: Verbs–Lie/Lay, Rise/Raise

Many writers have trouble with these tricky verb pairs. See whether you can beat the averages!

......................................**Did You Know?**..............................

The following word pairs have related meanings that invite confusion. Read on to learn how to use them correctly.

Lie **means "to be at rest or recline."** *Lay* **means "to put or to place (something)."**

> Beth just wanted to **lie** on the beach for a whole week.
> You should **lay** your beach towel on the sand away from the surf.

Rise **means "to move in an upward direction."** *Raise* **means "to lift (something)" or "to move something higher."**

> The moon should **rise** in the early evening, according to the script.
> Jenny tugged on the rope to **raise** the cutout moon in the theater set.

Show What You Know

Correctly fill in each blank with one of these words: *lie, lay, rise, raise.*

A Night in Camp

I am happy as I _____ on the air mattress, gazing at the brilliant, starry sky. I feel I
    1

could grab the low, oval moon and _____ it here beside me. Instead, I _____ very still.
                                   2   3

No noise disturbs the quiet. No breeze rustles the leaves above. Nearby, I see smoke _____
                                                                                       4

lazily from the dying campfire. It curls and twists up to the leafy ceiling of tree limbs.

Hypnotized, I watch it _____ higher and then disappear. When I _____ my head a
                        5   6

little, I see that the embers have at last died out. I want to wake up before dawn so that I can

see the sun _____. All is well in camp. This is the life!
             7

                                        Score: _____   **Total Possible: 7**

Proofread

The following bread recipe uses the verbs _lie/lay_ and _rise/raise_ incorrectly four times. Using the proper proofreading mark, delete each incorrect word and write the correct word above it.

Example: Does the cookbook ~~lay~~ ^lie^ on the table?

Della's Old-Fashioned Bread

1. Mix the yeast, sugar, and warm water in a small bowl. Put the bowl in a warm place for the

   yeast to raise.

2. In a separate bowl, mix the flour and salt. Lie this bowl aside for now.

3. After ten minutes, mix everything together in a large bowl. Make a ball of dough.

4. If the dough will lay in your hand without sticking, it is just right. If not, add flour.

5. Put the dough on your board. Rise your hand and push your palm into the dough. Raise your

   hand and repeat the action. (This action is called "kneading" the dough.)

Practice

Look at the drawing. What time of year does it suggest? Write a brief story or description in response to this picture. Use the verb pairs _lie/lay_ and _rise/raise_.

_____

_____

_____

_____

_____

_____

_____

_____

Tips for Your Own Writing: Proofreading

Choose a piece of your own writing. Look for the verbs _lie_ and _lay._ Check to see that _lie_ is used when you mean "to be at rest" and _lay_ when you mean "to put or place." Look for other troublesome word pairs such as _rise_ and _raise._

**D**on't lie down on the job, don't lay your troubles down, and don't raise your voice. Just rise to the occasion! Get it?

26 Usage: Verbs—Can/May, Let/Leave, Teach/Learn, Bring/Take

✏️ *With some confusing verb pairs, we just have to learn and remember the difference. It's hard work, but the payoff is appropriate usage!*

Did You Know?

The following word pairs have related meanings that invite confusion.

Can means "to be able to (do something)." *May* means "to be allowed or permitted to (do something)."

> **Incorrect:** "**Can** I be excused?" asked Carmen.
> **Correct:** "**May** I be excused?" asked Carmen.

Let means "to allow." *Leave* means "to depart" or "to permit something to remain where it is."

> **Incorrect:** "**Leave** me go!" begged the caged animal's eyes.
> **Correct:** "**Let** me go!" begged the caged animal's eyes.

Teach means "to explain" or "to help (someone) understand." *Learn* means "to gain knowledge."

> **Incorrect:** Please **learn** me how to tie a square knot.
> **Correct:** Please **teach** me how to tie a square knot.

Bring means "to fetch" or "to carry toward (oneself, something, or someone)." *Take* means "to carry in a direction away from (oneself, something, or someone)."

> **Incorrect: Bring** your mom to that countryside restaurant.
> **Correct: Take** your mom to that countryside restaurant.

Show What You Know

Underline the correct form of each verb in parentheses.

1. (Can, May) I speak six languages? Yes, (can, may) I show you now?

2. (Leave, Let) me just say this before I have to (leave, let).

3. Teachers want to (teach, learn) their pupils. Pupils want to (teach, learn) from them.

4. (Bring, Take) your lunch, but (take, bring) me the extra money.

Score: _____   Total Possible: 8

Proofread

The following report contains the verbs presented in this lesson. In six places, those verbs are used incorrectly. Using the proper proofreading mark, delete each incorrect word and write the correction above it.

Example: Let
~~Leave~~ us do the work.

The Chinese write their language in a different way than people write their languages in the West. They do not use an alphabet, if you may imagine that. Instead, the Chinese learn a unique character for every word. There are about fifty thousand characters in all. Imagine having to learn all those characters or having to learn them to someone else. In fact, educated Chinese can read thousands of characters. This knowledge will leave them read a newspaper easily.

Can I tell you one more thing? I am studying Chinese, and I will bring you to my class if you'd like. Just be sure to take an open mind with you.

Practice

Write one sentence for four of the verbs introduced in this lesson. Then use a dictionary to find definitions for these verbs that are different from the ones presented here. Write a sentence for each different definition you find.

_____

_____

_____

_____

_____

_____

_____

Tips for Your Own Writing: Proofreading..

The next time you write a story or report, be aware of how you can use *can* and *may.* Remember, *can* means "to be able to" and *may* means "to be allowed to."

*M*ay *I congratulate you on this lesson? You* can *now ace these difficult verbs!*

27 Review: Verbs

A. The following is a fictional account of an expedition to the South Pole. Underline the correct form of each verb in parentheses.

The expedition consisted of Woods, Danner, and Abaji, the captain. On December 1, the

crew (began, begun) its trek inland across the ice shelf. The first mishap occurred that very day.
　　　　　1

One of the dogs lost its footing and (fell, fallen) into the icy water. Though it (swam, swum) to
　　　　　　　　　　　　　　　　　2　　　　　　　　　　　　　　　　　　**3**

safety, the dog (shook, shaken) all over and was badly chilled. That night, the wind
　　　　　　　　4

(blew, blown) with a terrible force. Earlier, it had (blew, blown) down one of the tents in camp.
　5　　　　　　　　　　　　　　　　　　　　　　　　**6**

The crew soon learned that a gust had (tore, torn) this tent beyond repair. The very next day,
　　　　　　　　　　　　　　　　　　　　7

they watched helplessly as one of the supply sleds (sank, sunk) into a crevasse. Weighted down
　　　　　　　　　　　　　　　　　　　　　　　　8

with food, it had (sank, sunk) with terrifying speed. Hungry and engulfed by bitter cold, the
　　　　　　　9

party (fell, fallen) into despair.
　　10

Three days later, all but one had (froze, frozen) to death. This was Captain Abaji, who
　　　　　　　　　　　　　　　　11

(wrote, written) in his diary every day. His last entry was "We have (fell, fallen). Here I have
　12　　　　　　　　　　　　　　　　　　　　　　　　**13**

(wrote, written) the truth: we perished with courage."
　14

Score: _____　　　　**Total Possible: 14**

B. Decide whether the underlined word in each sentence is used correctly. If it is, put a **C** above the word. If it is not, write the correct word above the underlined word.

Brett had <u>stolen</u> a candy bar from his sister Ann's lunch box. He <u>taken</u> it without thinking
　　　　　1　　　　　　　　　　　　　　　　　　　　　　**2**

about his action. As he <u>torn</u> off the wrapper, he realized what he'd done. Though the candy
　　　　　　　　　　3

looked tasty, Brett <u>began</u> to feel very ashamed. He <u>wrote</u> a note of apology to put in Ann's
　　　　　　　　　4　　　　　　　　　　　**5**

lunch box with the candy bar. Just then, Ann came into the kitchen. Brett was <u>froze</u> in his tracks.
　　　　　　　　　　　　　　　　　　　　　　　　　　　　　　　6

Score: _____　　　　**Total Possible: 6**

C. In each blank, write a verb from the list. Some verbs may be used more than once. Some may not be used at all.

raise	rise	take	bring	let	leave	can	may	lie	lay

Clyde's Bad Break in Show Biz

MS. DÍAZ: Please _____ something to school for your demonstration speech.

        1

LOU: _____ I bring my pet snake Clyde? It will _____ quietly in one place and

      2   **3**

not bother a soul. We'll only have to worry if we see it _____ its tail.

                                                         4

MS. DÍAZ: But _____ your snake bite?

         5

LOU: Maybe. But I'll tell Clyde: "You _____ not bite!"

                                          6

MS. DÍAZ: Thanks, but I cannot _____ Clyde come to school. You will have to _____

                                7   **8**

your talented snake at home.

Score: _____   Total Possible: 8

D. Write the verb in the parentheses that correctly completes each sentence.

1. (rang, rung) The year is 1905. The school bell has just _____. The teacher _____

that bell by hand at the same time yesterday.

2. (teach, learn) The one-room schoolhouse is full of youngsters eager to _____. The

school has one teacher. She will _____ students of all ages.

3. (lie, lay) The students sit down and _____ their hands together on their desks. No one

will slouch or _____ down in this schoolroom!

4. (rise, raise) To ask a question, students must _____ their hands. The teacher says, "Yes,

Maude (or Clarence), you may _____."

5. (bring, take) There is no lunchroom. Students _____ cold food from home to school.

They _____ the leftovers home after the closing bell rings.

Score: _____   Total Possible: 10

REVIEW SCORE: _____   REVIEW TOTAL: 38

28 Usage: Adjectives

✏️ *Writing—and life—would be dull without comparisons. We have rules in English for how to compare using adjectives.*

Did You Know?

Adjectives—words that modify nouns or pronouns—use different forms when used to make comparisons. The comparative form of an adjective is used to compare two things.

> This fish is **larger** than that one.   Sara is **more talkative** than Li.

The superlative form of an adjective is used to compare more than two things.

> The Siberian tiger is the **largest** member of the cat family.
> The **most talkative** person I've ever known is Kareem.

Did you notice two of the adjectives end with *-er* or *-est* and the other two adjectives use *more* or *most*? Short adjectives usually add *-er* or *-est*. Longer adjectives usually add *more* or *most*.

Most adjectives are *regular:* they follow the above patterns in forming their comparatives and superlatives. But a few adjectives are *irregular:* they form their comparatives and superlatives in different ways.

Regular Adjectives	Comparative Adjectives	Superlative Adjectives
good	better	best
bad	worse	worst

The only way to learn these irregular forms is to memorize them.

Show What You Know

Rewrite each adjective in bold type. Write it in the blank in either the comparative or superlative form.

1. On the tennis court, Mei is a **powerful** opponent. Is she _____ than Jo?

2. But Jo has a **strong** backhand. It may be _____ than Mei's.

3. They are both **good** players. But which one is the _____ player?

4. Their match was a **long** one. It was the _____ match in the tournament.

5. It was also **exciting.** It was the _____ match I saw all week.

Score: _____   Total Possible: 5

Proofread

In the following report, underline the five adjectives that are used in their comparative or superlative form. For each of the four forms used incorrectly, use the proper proofreading mark to delete it and write the correction above it.

Example: A car moves ~~more slow~~ *slower* than a train.

The pyramid is a basic form in geometry. Human beings have built pyramids as tombs or places of worship throughout history. Of all the pyramids in the world, the taller one is King Khufu's Great Pyramid in Egypt. It rises more than 450 feet (137 meters). Some people consider this the beautifulest as well as the largest pyramid.

Native Americans also built many pyramids. American pyramids had a stair-stepped side and a flat top. The completest one today is the Temple of Inscriptions at Palenque, Mexico. Though quite beautiful, this structure is much more short than Egypt's Great Pyramid.

Practice

Write a story using at least five comparative or superlative adjectives.

_____

_____

_____

_____

_____

_____

_____

_____

_____

Tips for Your Own Writing: Proofreading..

The next time you write a description in a story, be sure you use -er or more with adjectives when comparing two things, and -est or most with adjectives when comparing more than two things.

When comparing two, use two letters (-er); when comparing three or more, use three letters (-est).

Lesson
29 Usage: Adverbs

 *A*dd spice to your writing with adverbs—especially adverbs of comparison.

························Did You Know?························

Adverbs—words that modify verbs, adjectives, or other adverbs—use different forms when used to make comparisons. The <u>comparative</u> form of an adverb is used to compare two actions.

> Deb arrived **later** than Heather.
> Bill shuffled his test papers **more noisily** than Tyrone.

The <u>superlative</u> form of an adverb is used to compare more than two actions.

> Jewel climbed the **highest** of all.
> Of all the students, Ernesto worked the **most rapidly.**

Short adverbs add *-er* or *-est.*

Most adverbs that end in *-ly* form their comparatives and superlatives using *more* and *most.* A few that do not end in *-ly* also use *more* and *most.*

> I eat olives **more often** than Mom, but Dad eats them the **most often.**

Most adverbs are *regular:* they follow the above patterns in forming their comparatives and superlatives. A few adverbs are *irregular.*

> Regular: The Badgers played **badly** in the play-offs.
> Comparative: The Tigers played **worse** than the Bears.
> Superlative: Of all the teams, the Lions played the **worst.**

Show What You Know

Rewrite the adverb in the bold type. Write it in the blank in either the comparative or superlative form.

1. Our hockey team skated **badly.** We skated _____ than we usually do.

2. The coach arrived at the rink **late.** The goalie arrived _____ of all.

3. Carl missed the goal **frequently.** He also shot _____ than others.

4. Our fans cheered **noisily.** Of all the schools' fans, we cheered the

_____.

Score: _____   Total Possible: 4

Proofread

In the following school newspaper article, underline the eight adverbs that are used in the comparative or superlative form. For the four forms used incorrectly, use the proper proofreading mark to delete the word and write the correction above it.

easier
Example: That race is ~~more easy~~ than this one.

The Science Club sponsored a Turtle Derby last Thursday. Three candidates—Ralph, Ed, and Trixie—lined up at the starting gate. At the pop of a balloon, they were off! Trixie moved slowly to start. But Ralph moved more slowly than Trixie. Ed moved the more slowly of the three. (It was clear that Trixie took the race seriouser than Ralph.)

When interviewed, a spectator, Perry Plum, said: "Trixie started badly, but Ed started worse
worst
than she did. Ralph started the ~~baddest~~ of the three." Not everyone agreed. Tilly Towson said, "I rate Trixie pretty high, Ed higher than Trixie, and Ralph the highest of all!"

So who won? The turtle who tried most hard—Trixie, of course.

Practice

Look at the picture. Write a description of the skier's run down the ski slope. Use at least two adverbs in their comparative or superlative form.

_____

_____

_____

_____

_____

_____

_____

_____

Tips for Your Own Writing: Revising

Choose a piece of your own writing. Exchange it with a partner to find the adverbs. Then, look for places to use adverbs that compare. Revise your writing.

*W*hat have you done superbly? *Then think of something you did* more superbly, *and finally, something you did the* most superbly *of all!*

30 Usage: Good/Well, Bad/Badly

Good and well *are as tangled as a plate of spaghetti! Read on to untangle them. (Thank goodness* bad *and* badly *are pretty straightforward.)*

....**Did You Know?**..

Good and *bad* are adjectives. Use them to modify nouns or pronouns. Sometimes they follow the verb. *Well* and *badly* are adverbs. Use them to modify verbs, adjectives, or other adverbs.

> I helped Raoul choose a **good** book.
> I feel **good** about the food we collected for homeless people.
> Mrs. Choy told me that Raoul read **well** in class.
> We had a **bad** thunderstorm last night.
> The weather forecaster predicted **badly**.

The word *well* is a special problem. It usually functions as an adverb, but it can be an adjective when it is used to mean "healthy." Usually, the adjective *well* follows a linking verb such as *am.*

> **Adverb:** Marita sang **well** at her concert last night.
> **Adjective:** "I am **well**," replied Ms. Slocum.

Remember that *good* is *always* used as an adjective. Also, remember that "feeling good" describes a state of mind, while "feeling well" describes someone's health.

....

Show What You Know

Underline the correct word in each word pair in parentheses.

Weightlessness is a potential health problem in space travel. Muscles can weaken

(bad, badly) if astronauts fail to exercise enough. Another (bad, badly) effect is that the heart
  1   **2**

may get larger. On the other hand, some astronauts say that weightlessness makes them feel

(good, badly). It brings on a mood of contentment. Scientists have found ways to help people
  3

cope with weightlessness. So, if you should meet an astronaut, ask, "How are you? Are you

(good, well) today?" Maybe she or he will answer, "I'm fine. I have coped (good, well) with
  4   **5**

weightlessness."

Score: _____   Total Possible: 5

Proofread

Bonita Bower's campaign speech has been published. It has five errors in it. Using the proper proofreading mark, delete each incorrect word and write the correction above it.

Example: The runner ran ~~good~~ *well* in the race.

Good evening. I'm running for mayor. During the last election, I was defeated bad. But since then, I have talked to many people from all walks of life. And I feel well about that. I've learned that we must all take an interest in city government.

I support conservation. As mayor, I will educate my staff to use supplies wisely. If we do good at this, I will not request an increase in office budgets for two years.

I also want to improve public transportation. Service isn't always very well. People who work far from home and don't drive are getting a badly deal.

Please vote for me, Bonita Bower, next Tuesday. I promise to do a good job!

Practice

Look at the picture. Have you ever thought about how difficult it must be to perform simple, daily tasks in space? Use your imagination to think of a way that this young astronaut could solve his problem. Use the word pairs introduced in this lesson.

_____

_____

_____

_____

_____

_____

_____

Tips for Your Own Writing: Proofreading..................................

Choose a piece of your own writing. Look for the words *good, well, bad,* and *badly.* Make sure that you used *good* and *bad* to describe nouns and pronouns, and *badly* to describe verbs, adjectives, and other adverbs. Pay particular attention to the word *well.*

 *D*id you do well *in this lesson? Then you should feel* good *about it!*

31 Usage: Accept/Except, Loose/Lose, Than/Then

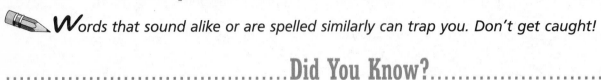 *W*ords *that sound alike or are spelled similarly can trap you. Don't get caught!*

......................................**Did You Know?**....................................

Because the following word pairs are similar in spelling and
pronunciation, writers tend to confuse them. Be careful to use each word
in the appropriate context.

Accept means "to take or receive (something)" or "to consent to
(something)." *Except* means "other than."

> I'd like to **accept** your invitation to address your computer club.
> Any day of the week **except** Monday is all right with me.

Loose means "not fastened" or "not tight." *Lose* means "to be unable to
find" or "to fail to keep."

> The chain has come **loose** from my bicycle's back wheel.
> The wheel wobbled and I started to **lose** my balance.

Than introduces the second part of a comparison. *Then* means "at that
time" or "afterward."

> New Jersey has a larger land area **than** Connecticut.
> We went to Connecticut, and **then** we went to New Jersey.

Show What You Know

**Underline the word in parentheses that correctly completes each sentence in the paragraphs
below.**

"I (accept, except) the challenge," responded the game-show contestant. "Just this one
$\quad$ 1

try, and (than, then) I'll stop."
$\quad$ 2

The host read the question: "What nations have more land (than, then) the U.S.? Uh-oh. I
$\quad$ 3

think Rachel's microphone came (loose, lose). Let's try again. Rachel? (Buzzer.) The correct
$\quad$ 4

answer is Russia, (than, then) Canada, (than, then) China. So sorry, Rachel, but you
$\quad$ 5 $\qquad$ 6

(loose, lose). You won't get any prizes, (accept, except) the play-at-home game."
7 $\qquad$ 8

Score: _____   Total Possible: 8

62

Proofread

The following story contains words presented in this lesson. Five of them are used incorrectly. Using the proper proofreading mark, delete each incorrect word and write the correction above it.

Example: I ~~except~~ your invitation.
accept

One day, Lucy's pet parakeet flew away. After two weeks of looking for it, Lucy's mom

told her that she'd have to except her loss. "It is painful to loose a pet like Teresa," said Lucy

sadly. "I should never have let her loose from her cage."

Than one day Lucy was visiting her cousin Dee in a nearby town. They heard a "tap, tap,

tap" on the kitchen window. Dee exclaimed, "I believe it's Teresa!"

Dee's mom said, "This is the wildest pet story I've ever heard."

"Accept for Juan's snake story," suggested Dee. "Juan claimed that when

his pet snake got lose, it came out of the wall in his neighbor's

apartment!"

Practice

Write sentences for each of the word pairs presented in this lesson. Use your imagination to create interesting sentences.

_____

_____

_____

_____

_____

_____

_____

_____

Tips for Your Own Writing: Proofreading.....................................

Scan a piece of your writing looking for the words in this lesson. Use *then* for "next"—*than* for "compare"; *accept* for "receive"—*except* for "not"; *loose* for "not tight"—*lose* for "no win."

Lesson

32 Usage: Principle/Principal, There/They're/Their, Its/It's

Homophones are words that sound alike but have different spellings and meanings. The words in this lesson are homophones.

...............................Did You Know?..............................

Because the following words sound the same and look alike, writers tend to confuse them. Context is the best clue as to which word to use in a sentence.

Principle means "a basic rule or belief." *Principal* means "most important" or "main." It also means "the chief or main person."

> This science experiment demonstrates the **principle** of inertia.
> Mrs. Monetti's **principal** objection was the noise.
> Mrs. Monetti is the **principal** of our school.

There means "at that place." *They're* is a contraction for "they are." *Their* means "belonging to them."

> The people in Lake Landis really like it **there.**
> **They're** having a wonderful festival in July.
> Have you seen **their** brochure for the festival?

Its is the possessive form of *it. It's* is a contraction for "it is."

> The bird fluffed up **its** feathers.
> You know **it's** going to be a cold day.

Show What You Know

Underline the word in parentheses that correctly completes each sentence in the paragraph below.

Today I'll demonstrate the (principle, principal) of osmosis. (Its, It's) the
                                    1   2
(principle, principal) lesson that we'll cover this week. Osmosis is the movement of one solution
        3
to another when (they're, their) separated by a membrane. A plant absorbs most of (its, it's)
                        4   5
water by the process of osmosis. Would the lab groups please pick up (there, their) notebooks
                                                                          6
and follow me? If you will gather around Table 2, you will see that a demonstration is set up

(there, their).
    7

Score: _____   Total Possible: 7

Proofread

In Talia's report, use the proper proofreading mark to delete each of the six incorrect words and write the correction above it.

Example: They forgot ~~there~~ *their* books.

Dragonflies are among the most beautiful insects. Because their principle food is insects,

their helpful, too. They can eat there own weight in insects in a half hour.

It's hard to believe, but a dragonfly lives almost it's entire life in a wingless form called a

nymph. The beautiful, gauzy-winged flier that we know represents only a few weeks to a few

months of this insect's life. Dragonflies live for several years.

No insect can fly as fast as a dragonfly. They're are reports of these fliers darting as fast

as a car on the highway—60 mph! No wonder they can catch so many insects.

Some extinct ancestors of today's dragonfly were huge. They

had wingspans of almost three feet. Its hard to imagine that!

Practice

Look at the picture. How would you react to seeing a giant dragonfly? Write a description of this dragonfly as if you were seeing it in real life. Try to use the words introduced in this lesson.

_____

_____

_____

_____

_____

_____

_____

Tips for Your Own Writing: Proofreading....................................

Search for any of these troublesome words—*principal/principle, there/they're/their, its/it's*—in a piece of your own writing. Determine whether you have used the words correctly.

Don't forget the apostrophe! It's a small mark, but its presence can make all the difference.

33 Review: Adjectives, Adverbs

A. **In the following movie review, underline the correct form of the adjective in each set of parentheses.**

For a *really* (good, best) film, see *Danada Square* by director George Chan. It is a
1
(more sentimental, sentimentaler) movie than Chan's previous film, *Run Home! Danada Square*
2
tells the story of a young Asian-American woman who starts a business in a shopping center.

She encounters many difficulties, including prejudice. But the (baddest, worst) part of all her
3
troubles is conflict with the landlord of her store. Of course, this (bad, worst) person is the
4
villain of the movie. Of Chan's four films, I think that this is the (goodest, best) one.
5

On the other hand, *Damage in Kuala Lumpur* is the (baddest, worst) movie I've seen in
6
years. It's a disaster movie about three high-rise towers in that Asian capital. The (taller, tallest)
7
of the three, called the "Black Tower," has a bomb scare. Then the "Green Tower," which is

(taller, tallest) than the "White Tower," catches fire. So it goes. Stay away from this movie and
8
save your money!

Score: _____   Total Possible: 8

B. **In each sentence in the paragraph below, underline the correct form of the adverb in parentheses.**

Ziggy Zales hit (low, more low) in yesterday's opening match. He hits the
1
(most low, lowest) of any tennis player that I can recall. Laura Farfone delivers the
2
(most fast, fastest) serve of any tennis player. Her serve is definitely (fast, faster) than that of
3   4
champion Maria Rivera. Some people think tennis moves (more quickly, quicklier) than baseball.
5
Laura slept (badly, bad) before the tennis match. But Ziggy slept (more badly, worse) than
6   7
Laura.

Score: _____   Total Possible: 7

C. Choose the word from the parentheses that correctly completes each sentence and write it in the blank.

1. The defense attorneys were certain that their case was very _____. (strong, strongly)

2. "I _____ object!" exclaimed the lawyer. (strong, strongly)

3. The main witness for the defense related a _____ story. (sad, sadly)

4. She _____ wiped her tears away, which was a nice touch. (sad, sadly)

5. The attorney wants a _____ conclusion to this trial. (prompt, promptly)

6. "The court will reconvene _____ at ten o'clock," said Judge Wu. (prompt, promptly)

Score: _____   Total Possible: 6

D. Read Marla's report on "Weird Planets." There are twelve errors. Using the proper proofreading mark, delete each incorrect word and write the correction above it.

The more we know about the principle planets in our solar system, the more normal our planet Earth seems. Earth has eight planet cousins, and their really weird!

Consider Mercury, the planet closest to the sun. A day on Mercury is 88 Earth days long. One side of Mercury faces the sun for 88 days in a row, getting bad burned at 800°F. The opposite, shady side must loose heat for those 88 days. Its frigid!

Saturn is beautiful, accept it is deadly. It has the largest and most visible rings, which circle it's middle like a belt. You wouldn't want to vacation their: Saturn's winds blow at speeds of 1,000 mph. That's about five times faster then a severe tornado's winds.

But the weirdest planet is Uranus. This planet violates the principal by which the other planets rotate like tops. Instead, Uranus spins oddly on its side. (If I were Uranus, I wouldn't feel very good after eons of this motion.) Uranus should except the "weirdest planet" award!

Score: _____   Total Possible: 12

REVIEW SCORE: _____   REVIEW TOTAL: 33

34 Usage: Plural Nouns

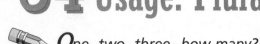

One, two, three—how many? Two or more means "use the plural."

······················**Did You Know?**······················

A singular noun names one person, place, thing, or idea. A plural noun names two or more persons, places, things, or ideas.

Plural nouns are formed in the following ways:

- **most nouns, add -s.**

    girl**s**   friend**s**

- **nouns ending in s, sh, ch, or x, add -es.**

    box**es**   church**es**

- **nouns ending in y preceded by a consonant, change y to i and add -es.**

    body—bod**ies**

- **nouns ending in y preceded by a vowel, add just -s.**

    toy—toy**s**   boy—boy**s**

- **some nouns ending in o, add -s. Some ending in o preceded by a consonant, add -es.**

    radio**s**   echo**es**

- **many nouns ending in f or fe, change the f to v and add -es or -s. Some nouns ending in f, add only -s.**

    calf—cal**ves**
    knife—kni**ves**
    chief—chief**s**

- **a few nouns, make no change between the singular and plural.**

    sheep   moose

- **a few nouns form the plural irregularly.**

    goose—geese
    child—children

··

Show What You Know

Write the plurals of the underlined words on the lines.

1. the echo of two banjo   _____

2. recipe: ten ripe cherry and two tomato   _____

3. some essay challenge your belief   _____

4. the report "Wolf and Fox"   _____

5. a new play, "Do Sheep Have Tooth?"   _____

Score: _____   **Total Possible: 10**

Proofread

Read Dino's story. He has formed seven plurals incorrectly. Using the proper proofreading mark, delete each incorrect plural and write the correct word above it.

Example: I read three ~~storys~~ _{stories} today.

My friendes and I wanted to have a computer club. We're crazy about computeres. We started inviting everyone we thought would like to join. We decided not to have a president because we don't like the idea of having bosses. Instead, we have two chieves: a chief program chairperson and a chief refreshment chair. They will have no vetos over club decisiones.

Thinking up a clever name wasn't easy. In the end, we chose "Torpedos." Why? Because sometimes torpedos come after you, figuratively speaking, when you carelessly key in a mistake!

Practice

Write a brief story about an afternoon "lineup" on the radio. Include plural nouns in your writing.

_____

_____

_____

_____

_____

_____

_____

_____

Tips for Your Own Writing: Proofreading.................................

If a plural form you want to use in your writing is not shown in this lesson, look the noun up in the dictionary. Most dictionaries list irregular plurals. Otherwise, add *-s* or *-es* to the noun.

Adding -s is a good bet for forming a plural, but it won't always be right.

35 Usage: Possessive Nouns

It's mine! It's mine! Possessive nouns show ownership.

......................................Did You Know?....................................

A possessive noun shows ownership of a noun that follows. Remember: a noun is a word that names a person, place, thing, or idea.

The following rules show how to form the possessive of nouns:

If the noun is singular, add an apostrophe and *s*.

> I'm going to my sister**'s** new office.
> Cass**'s** job is public relations director of the national fair.

If the noun is plural and ends in *s*, add an apostrophe only.

> This national fair is the cities**'** showcase.

If the noun is plural and does not end in *s*, add an apostrophe and *s*.

> The fair has a children**'s** pavilion.

Show What You Know

On the line, write the correct possessive form of each underlined noun.

1. <u>birds</u> adaptations for flight   _____

2. a <u>bird</u> wing   _____

3. an <u>ostrich</u> story   _____

4. an <u>ibis</u> story   _____

5. <u>owls</u> quiet hunting flights   _____

6. <u>mice</u> chances when a hawk is near   _____

Score: _____   **Total Possible: 6**

Proofread

Read Marianne's report. Using the proper proofreading mark, delete each of the five incorrect possessive nouns and write the correction above it.

Example: What is your ~~cousins's~~ *cousin's* name?

In ancient Greece, many myths were told and later written down. One such myth is about Icarus, who was Daedalus' son. Daedalus was a marvelous builder and inventor. But he had been imprisoned in a maze for a crime. Daedalus saw a way to escape. He made wings for himself out of birds's feathers and some wax. Using the wings, Daedalus was able to fly out of the maze.

Icarus was so excited by the wings's power and the thrill of flying that he ignored his father's warning. He used his fathers wings and flew higher and higher. He got too close to the suns burning rays and melted the wax that held together his wings. He fell to his death.

Practice

Look at the picture. Imagine that you are the rabbit and that you are being hunted by the owl. What emotions would you feel? What strategies would you devise to outwit this bird of prey? Write a paragraph of the rabbit's thoughts below. Use some possessive nouns in your paragraph.

_____

_____

_____

_____

_____

_____

_____

Tips for Your Own Writing: Proofreading ....

Choose something you have written recently. Check any possessive nouns you used to make sure you have used apostrophes correctly.

 You've done another day's *work. Or is it two* days' *work?*

36 Usage: Contractions

Here's a hint for identifying contractions: look for the apostrophe and see whether any letters have been omitted.

.... Did You Know? ....

A **contraction** is a word formed by combining two words and omitting one or more letters. We show the omission of letters by inserting an apostrophe. One type of contraction combines a pronoun and verb.

she + is = she's	I + am = I'm
who + is = who's	we + are = we're
I + have = I've	he + will = he'll
you + have = you've	they + will = they'll

Another type of contraction combines a verb and the negative word *not*.

are + not = aren't   will + not = won't

Do not confuse contractions with possessive pronouns. For example, the contraction *you're* sounds like the possessive pronoun *your*.

You're sorry that you lost **your** videocassette.

Show What You Know

In the paragraph below, write the contraction for each underlined word or group of words above the word or words.

We are disturbed about plans for the new superhighway. It is supposed to cut through the
___1___   ___2___

forest preserve. If the road is built, some animal populations will not survive. They cannot
                                                                ___3___   ___4___

tolerate the increased noise and air pollution. We have formed a citizen committee to work for
                                                 ___5___

a change. Who is interested in becoming a member? I am in charge of next month's meeting.
         ___6___   ___7___

Please do not forget to sign our petition before you leave.
       ___8___

Score: _____   **Total Possible: 8**

72

Proofread

Read the following tour guide to a historic house. Help the editors make seven corrections. Using the proper proofreading mark, delete each incorrect contraction and write the correction above it.

Example: I'll be home by dark.

Welcome to the Elisa Bentley house. Wont you come in? You're   first stop is the vestibule,

a small entry room. Notice the hand-painted wallpaper from about the 1800s. Its' really quite

rare. Next, youll enter the formal parlor. Of course, this house had no electricity, and w'eve

tried to preserve that feeling by using low lighting. Notice the Regency style of decoration.

Is'nt it exquisite! The master bedroom is next. Here we'l see a hand-carved, four-poster bed.

Ms. Bentley was most particular about the condition of her bed. Please return to the front of

the house. Your tour has ended.

Practice

Imagine that you will write a guide for your room or some other room that you know well. Follow these steps:

1. Allow yourself time to walk through the room (at least in your mind) and notice details.

2. Decide which details are worth writing about and which ones should be left out.

3. Write the guide to the room just as if you were walking around it, noticing the details.

_____

_____

_____

_____

_____

Tips for Your Own Writing: Proofreading

Remember that a contraction stands for two words. It must have an apostrophe. A possessive pronoun never uses an apostrophe.

 If you'll try hard, you won't fail to understand contractions.

37 Review: Plurals, Possessives, Contractions

A. **In each sentence, form the plural of the word in parentheses and write it in the blank to complete the sentence.**

1. Today's _____ have a wide variety of software. (computer)

2. Our software usually comes in _____ that we call *packages.* (box)

3. You can play many _____ on the computer. (game)

4. My screen saver shows little _____ gliding through the water. (torpedo)

5. I've also seen screen savers that show _____ exploding. (tomato)

6. Many people used to regard computers as _____. (toy)

7. But _____ in offices find that software makes workers productive. (boss)

8. Software can teach you fingering for _____ or tuning for pianos. (banjo)

9. Some do-it-yourself packages tell how to repair _____ on houses. (roof)

10. Packages even instruct _____ on building thermal homes. (beginner)

11. And some packages tell farmers how to raise calves and _____! (goose)

12. You could probably tell many more _____ about unusual software. (story)

Score: _____   Total Possible: 12

B. **In the paragraph below, write the possessive form of each underlined word above it.**

I couldn't help laughing at <u>Dad</u> accident. He dabbed red paint on both of his <u>sleeves</u> cuffs.
        1   2

He "had a <u>sheep</u> face"—meaning he looked sheepish. I couldn't wait to see the <u>kids</u> reaction
            3   4

when they came in. "It was my <u>hands</u> fault," said Dad. "They're clumsy."
                                5

Score: _____   Total Possible: 5

C. Read this explanation of the naming of the computer object we call a *mouse.* If an underlined possessive or plural noun is used correctly, write **C** above it. Otherwise, write the correction there.

Have you wondered where computer <u>objects'</u> names come from? A *bug* is so named
$\qquad$ **1**

because a real insect interrupted several <u>circuits</u> electron flow in an early computer. But
$\qquad$ **2**

perhaps the <u>mouses</u> name is the most humorous. It's not difficult to guess the <u>name's</u> origin.
$\qquad$ **3** $\qquad$ **4**

A <u>computers</u> mouse has a long "tail" and a smooth, rounded shape. How strange it would be
$\qquad$ **5**

if the computer mouse looked like a goose. Would we now have "<u>geese-driven</u>" software
$\qquad$ **6**

programs?

Score: _____   Total Possible: 6

D. Read the following science report. It contains eight errors. Using the proper proofreading mark, delete each incorrect contraction and write the correction above it.

Large birds of prey are very territorial. This means that they wont tolerate other large birds

living nearby, especially if the other birds' diets are similar to theirs. They want to avoid

competition with the other birds.

Large crows and owls, for example, do not mix well. The spring is an especially tough

time of year, because their trying to raise their young. If youre lucky enough to live in an

uncrowded area that has many large trees, you may see this bird drama played out above

you're own head.

Large owls are very powerful creatures, and most birds dont bother them. But crows are

very social—this means that they're accustomed to living closely with each other. And they rely

on each other, too. When crows feel threatened, theyl'l call all other crows within earshot.

(Wer'e used to the sound of crows. They're very noisy birds.) In this way, many crows can

gang up on an owl. In the end, its quite possible for the crows to win.

Score: _____   Total Possible: 8

REVIEW SCORE: _____   REVIEW TOTAL: 31

38 Usage: Simple Past Tense

"It was the best of times, it was the worst of times." How do we tell about things that happened in the past?

.... **Did You Know?** ....

Tenses of verbs tell whether an action or a state of being took place in the past, the present, or the future.

We use the past tense of a verb to talk or write about something that happened in the past. The simple past tense consists of one word that describes a past action. Many verbs form the simple past tense by adding -d or -ed to the present tense.

Present Tense	Simple Past Tense
Today they ask.	Yesterday they ask**ed.**
Today they play.	Yesterday they play**ed.**
Today they climb.	Yesterday they climb**ed.**

Other verbs form the simple past tense irregularly: sometimes by changing spellings, sometimes by not changing at all.

Present Tense	Simple Past Tense	Present Tense	Simple Past Tense
make	made	buy	bought
choose	chose	drink	drank
know	knew	hit	hit
feel	felt	cut	cut

....

Show What You Know

In the blank, write the correct past tense of the verb in parentheses to complete the sentence.

1. Clara _____ to paint her house this summer. (decide)

2. The store manager _____ a good brand of paint. (recommend)

3. Then Clara _____ many cans of that paint. (buy)

4. Next, she _____ the old paint off the exterior of her house. (scrape)

5. To reach the high spots, she carefully _____ on a strong ladder. (climb)

6. Then Clara _____ the paint on the outside walls. (brush)

7. That evening she _____ her freshly painted home. (admire)

Score: _____   Total Possible: 7

Proofread

Using the proper proofreading mark, delete each of the twelve incorrect past-tense verbs and write the correct word above it.

                            asked
Example: Yesterday I was ~~ask~~ to a party.

Last May our town celebrated its centennial, or one-hundredth, anniversary. We maked a lot of preparations. A cleanup committee wash and brushd all public buildings. Members of the fire department clumb on high ladders to put up flags and bunting.

At last the celebration started. The high point was when Mayor Lopez askt Olga Janssen— at 105, our oldest citizen—what she rememberd about the old days. "How I usd a churn to make butter and playd dominoes with my cousins," said Mrs. Janssen.

At the end, we all drunk a ginger ale toast to the town's next century. We knowed most of us wouldn't be here for the next celebration, but we feeled happy to be at this one. To officially close our celebration, the mayor hitted a large bell with a mallet.

Practice

Rewrite the story in Show What You Know, describing Clara's painting experience. Add descriptive details. When the story is finished, underline all the past-tense verbs.

_____

_____

_____

_____

_____

_____

_____

Tips for Your Own Writing: Proofreading...

If you need help with past-tense verbs, use the dictionary. A dictionary entry for an irregular verb usually lists the past-tense form right after the main entry. For any verbs that give you trouble, write them in your journal or writing folder where you can find them easily.

 The only time you can control time is when you change verb tense!

39 Usage: Subject-Verb Agreement I

You don't want your subjects and verbs to fight with each other. Make sure they agree!

......Did You Know?......

The present tense form of a verb is used to talk or write about something that is happening now. In the present tense of most verbs, the only form that changes is the one used with *he, she,* **or** *it.* **This form adds either** *-s* **or** *-es.* **By using the appropriate form of the verb with the subject, we make the subject and verb agree in number. A verb with an** *-s* **ending is used with** *he, she, it,* **or other singular subjects, and a verb without an** *-s* **ending is used with all other subjects.**

A conjugation is a table of the forms that a verb takes in a particular tense. Below are conjugations of two verbs in the present tense.

Present Tense of *Live*		Present Tense of *Fix*	
I live	we live	I fix	we fix
you live	you live	you fix	you fix
he, she, it live**s**	they live	he, she, it fix**es**	they fix

Most verbs ending in *s, sh,* **or** *ch* **add** *-es* **in the present form for** *he, she,* **or** *it.*

Show What You Know

If the subject and verb in each sentence agree, put a *C* above the underlined verb. If they do not agree, write the correct present-tense form of the verb above the underlined verb.

1. My older sister Karin <u>fixes</u> cars.

2. She washes and <u>wax</u> them, too, for a small fee.

3. Karin <u>works</u> on cars most Saturdays.

4. She often <u>start</u> working at 7:00 in the morning.

5. Mom isn't very good with cars, so she sometimes <u>watch</u> Karin.

6. Karin only <u>wish</u> she could make more money fixing cars.

7. I think Karin is too busy. She <u>dash</u> from one thing to another.

8. I think she <u>try</u> to do too much between school and her job.

Score: _____   Total Possible: 8

Proofread

Rick's report, entitled "How We Depend on Electricity," has five verbs and subjects that do not agree. Using the proper proofreading mark, delete the verb in each error of agreement. Above it, write the verb form that corrects the agreement problem.

Example: That dog ~~bark~~ <u>barks</u> too much.

We often don't realize how much we depend on electricity until it stop. When lightning

flashes or a powerful wind blow down a power line, we're in trouble!

Want to watch TV or listen to that new CD? Not without electricity. Think you'll have

some dinner? Try it cold. The family member who fix the food will love doing without a stove.

You'd like to read a book? Read while the candle melt!

You feel so thankful when the power come on again. How did

people live without it?

Practice

Look at the picture. It shows one way family and friends entertained themselves at night before electricity. Imagine that you will have to live for a period of several weeks or months without electricity. How will you entertain yourself and others? How will you cope with the nighttime darkness? Write a short description of what you would do.

_____

_____

_____

_____

_____

_____

_____

Tips for Your Own Writing: Proofreading..

Select a piece of your own writing and look for verbs in the present tense. Check for agreement with the subject. Just remember: the verb adds *-s* or *-es* when the subject is *he, she, it,* or any singular noun.

 Subjects and verbs that work together make strong sentences.

40 Usage: Subject-Verb Agreement II

Where's the subject? Where's the verb? If you can answer these questions, you're a long way toward understanding this lesson.

......................................**Did You Know?**......................................

There are some special problems of agreement between subjects and verbs. In most cases, the subject comes before the verb. However, sometimes we invert, or reverse the order of, subjects and verbs to make a sentence more interesting.

> Out of the fog **rises** the **castle**.

Sentences that begin with *here, there,* and *where* put the subject after the verb.

> Here **is** the **drawbridge**.
> Where **are** the **gates?**

Sometimes a prepositional phrase comes between the subject and the verb.

> A **knight** with many servants **arrives** at the castle.

A *compound subject* is made of two or more nouns or pronouns. Compound subjects joined by *and* always take a verb that does not end in -s. If the verb is irregular, use the form for plural subjects with a compound subject.

> The **knight and** his **squire are** attending the tournament.

Compound subjects joined by *or* or *nor* take a form of the verb that agrees with the subject nearest to the verb.

> Either the queen or **her servants have** the secret key.

....

Show What You Know

If the subject and verb in each sentence agree, put a *C* above the underlined verb. If they do not, write the correct present-tense form of the verb above the underlined verb.

Where <u>is</u> evidence of the Ice Age in North America? Many U.S. states and Canadian
₁

provinces <u>show</u> such evidence. Objects under a glacial mass <u>forms</u> various land features.
₂ ₃

Moraines and eskers <u>are</u> types of glacial deposits. From glacial ice <u>come</u> most of the fresh
₄ ₅

water on Earth. Glaciers <u>ranges</u> in thickness from 300 to 10,000 feet.
₆

Score: _____   Total Possible: 6

Proofread

Following is a report Tara wrote after a field trip with her science class. Find the six errors of subject-verb agreement. Using the proper proofreading mark, delete each incorrect word and write the correction above it.

Example: There ~~is~~ ^{are} five science books on the table.

About twenty thousand years ago, the last glacier of the most recent Ice Age retreated

northward. As a result, many glacial formations dots our fertile farmlands. Everywhere is low

mounds covered with trees. These mounds in each area tells a story. On some of them grows

no crops. Farmers don't always plows the rougher, rockier soil of the glacial mounds. Glaciers

have also left behind kettle lakes. A kettle is a bowl-like depression. It remains after a huge

chunk of glacial ice has melted. Terminal moraines—long, hilly ridges—also mark the end of

glaciers. You can see one if you follow Route 77 westward from Barrytown. But neither kettles

nor terminal moraines tells the entire story of glaciers in the Ice

Age. For the whole story, you'll have to study geology.

Practice

Write a paragraph describing the terrain, or land formation, in your area. Is it flat, hilly, or coastal? What kind of vegetation covers the land? Be careful about subject-verb agreement.

_____

_____

_____

_____

_____

Tips for Your Own Writing: Proofreading...

The next time you write a story or report, try using some compound subjects. If you join the subjects with *and,* use a verb form that does not end in *-s.* If the subjects are joined by *or* or *nor,* use a verb form that agrees with the nearest subject.

 To make verbs and subjects agree, first identify the verbs and the subjects.

41 Review: Past Tense Verbs, Subject-Verb Agreement

A. In the blank in each sentence, write the past tense of the verb in parentheses.

1. Jamal's teacher _____ him to perform in the piano recital. (ask)

2. He _____ a piece by Chopin called "Valse Brilliante." (choose)

3. When Jamal walked onto the stage, he _____ very nervous. (feel)

4. He _____ the beginning of his piece, but not the ending. (remember)

5. As Jamal _____ the keys, he felt more confident. (touch)

6. He _____ every single note perfectly. (hit)

7. At the reception, everyone said, "Jamal, you _____ very well." (play)

Score: _____   Total Possible: 7

B. In the blank, write the correct ending (*s* or *es*) for each incomplete verb. The completed verb should agree in number with its subject.

    Tornadoes are fantastically powerful whirlwinds. A tornado form_____ along a front, or
₁

narrow zone, between a mass of cool, dry air and a mass of warm, very humid air. The warm,

moist air rise_____ in rapid updrafts. Soon, a column of air spin_____. If the updraft is
₂   ₃

powerful enough, it feed_____ the growing tornado. Air rush_____ up the column.
₄   ₅

    Soon a funnel drop_____ down from the sky. It touch_____ down, raising a black
₆   ₇

dust cloud. A tornado toss_____ about debris like paper. It sometimes pitch_____
₈   ₉

automobiles or tractors like softballs. Tornadoes would seem like pranksters if they weren't so

violent. A twister sometimes levels houses on one side of a street but miss_____ those on
₁₀

the other side completely. The narrow, whirling column pass_____ close to some objects
₁₁

without harming them. Thank goodness the average tornado live_____ for only a few
₁₂

minutes!

Score: _____   Total Possible: 12

C. In each pair of verbs in parentheses, underline the verb that agrees in number with the subject.

Out of the shadows (step, steps) the king's herald. "I declare, according to His Majesty's
                    1
will," he cries, "that from this day forward the queen and her retinue shall be kept under

guard in the palace." Through the crowd (run, runs) a low murmur.
                                         2

But where (is, are) the key to the secret passage under the palace? Does the queen have
          3
it? No, Prince Renaldo (possess, possesses) it. He and Princess Angelina (plot, plots) to aid
                        4   **5**
the queen.

What is the climax of our story? The queen and her servants (makes, make) their escape.
                                                            6
Neither the officials of the court nor the king (find, finds) a way to stop them. Into the free
                                                7
light and air they (walk, walks).
                    8

Score: _____   Total Possible: 8

D. Fill in each blank with *is, are, was,* or *were* so that the subject and the verb agree in tense and number.

Asteroids are rocky chunks that orbit the sun in space. Sometimes an asteroid comes into

Earth's atmosphere and becomes a meteor. Usually, a meteor vaporizes in the atmosphere. We

call the objects that do reach the ground *meteorites*. There _____ evidence that
                                                          1
meteorites have slammed into Earth. They have left very large craters. In a few cases, there

_____ surviving meteorites, too.
2

Meteorites can be very destructive. Scientists believe that there _____ a huge
                                                                  3
meteorite above Siberia in 1908. It apparently exploded in the air, flattening and burning

forests. Remember that there _____ once dinosaurs on Earth. Some scientists think that a
                            4
massive meteorite hit Earth and raised so much dust that it changed the climate, killing off the

dinosaurs. Here _____ something to think about: What would happen if a very large
                5
asteroid was predicted to hit Earth very soon?

Score: _____   Total Possible: 5

REVIEW SCORE: _____   REVIEW TOTAL: 32

42 Usage: Pronouns—Agreement and Order I

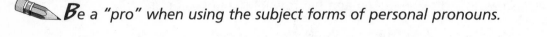 *Be a "pro" when using the subject forms of personal pronouns.*

Did You Know?

Personal pronouns have subject forms and object forms, in addition to singular, plural, and possessive forms.

The subject form of a pronoun is used as the subject of the sentence or as a pronoun following a linking verb.

A subject pronoun can be used as the subject of the sentence.

> **He** drew the illustrations in the book.

A subject pronoun can be used after a linking verb. You can decide what form of the pronoun to use by inverting the sentence.

> The author of the book was **she.**/**She** was the author of the book.

Show What You Know

Read the paragraphs. In each set of parentheses, underline the correct subject pronoun.

In 1804–1806, Captains Meriwether Lewis and William Clark led an expedition across the territory of Louisiana. Today (we, us) know this vast region as the Northern Plains of
¹
northwestern U.S.

One woman accompanied the crew—Sacagawea. The courageous daughter of a Shoshone was (she, her). Because Sacagawea helped with communication, the explorers were able to
²
find horses and guides.

The explorers learned much about landforms, wildlife, and Native Americans. (They, Them) spent their first winter in camp with the Mandan and later met the Nez Percé in the northern
³
Rockies. Finally, in November 1805, the expedition reached the Pacific Ocean. (It, Its) was an
⁴
astonishing sight, according to Captain Clark.

Score: _____   Total Possible: 4

Proofread

This imaginary newspaper editorial of 1806 speculates that the members of the Lewis and Clark expedition are lost or dead. The writer used four personal pronouns incorrectly. Draw a delete mark through each mistake and write the correction above it.

Example: ~~Us~~ *We* have received no mail from them.

We fear that the noble expedition of Captains Lewis and Clark has failed. Consider how many conditions were against they. The party was last heard from one year ago, when Corporal Warfington rowed into St. Louis. He was a member of the expedition. Since that time, us have received no word. Yet our ears heard rumors of capture by Spaniards. Some think them suffered an even worse fate. Whatever the truth about the noble explorers, heroes were them all.

Practice

Imagine that you are a member of an exploration party in an unknown territory. Write the body of a letter to someone back home—a family member, friend, reporter, or the President. Tell a story about some challenge you have faced. Use at least four subject pronouns.

_____

_____

_____

_____

_____

_____

_____

_____

Tips for Your Own Writing: Proofreading...

In a piece of your own writing, check the forms of the pronouns you used. To choose the correct pronoun form, identify how the pronoun functions in each sentence. If a pronoun is used as a subject or after a linking verb, use the subject form of the pronoun.

 The subject of this lesson is subject pronouns as subjects.

43 Usage: Pronouns—Agreement and Order II

Be clear about the uses of object pronouns: as direct objects, indirect objects, and objects of prepositions.

Personal pronouns have singular and plural subject forms, object forms, and possessive forms.

An object pronoun can be used as a <u>direct object</u> of a verb. Notice that a direct object usually comes after the verb and tells what the verb acted upon.

> Because Anne's cookies are delicious, she is taking **them** to the bake sale.

An object pronoun can be used as an <u>indirect object</u> in a sentence. Notice that the indirect object comes between the verb and the direct object (*cake*). It tells to or for whom the verb acted. A direct object is necessary in a sentence with an indirect object.

> Jim bakes **her** a cake for the birthday party.

An object pronoun can be used as the <u>object of a preposition</u>. Notice that the object of a preposition comes after the preposition *for*.

> Ted and Lisa bake bread for **us.**

Show What You Know

Tell how each underlined personal pronoun is used. Is it a direct object, an indirect object, or the object of a preposition? Write DO, IO, or OP above each underlined personal pronoun.

1. "I'll splatter <u>you</u> with this pie," joked the clown.

2. "Go ahead, entertain <u>us</u>," dared the audience member.

3. "The Great Miranda" performed for <u>them</u>.

4. "Give <u>me</u> the ticket," said the lady at the circus box office.

5. Amazing Amanda the magician sawed <u>him</u> in half.

6. "I think we pleased <u>them</u>," said the master of ceremonies.

7. "We always give <u>them</u> their money's worth."

Score: _____   Total Possible: 7

Proofread

The following music review uses seven personal pronouns incorrectly. Draw a delete mark through each incorrect word and write the correction above it.

Example: Please find a seat for ~~we~~. *us*

    The City Philharmonic played a dazzling concert last night. The conductor was pleased, and so was I. The audience agreed with he and I. Mellow as ever, the string section soothed and inspired we. The horns blared and bounced with agility. (Give they a hand!) The single brass player blasted his trumpet. (Hats off to he!) But best of all, percussion player Sara Hue punctuated just the right moments. The audience gave she a standing ovation! Between you and I, I think it was one of the orchestra's best concerts ever.

Practice

Write five sentences describing a live performance or movie that you have attended or seen recently. It could be a concert, a sports event, a movie, or a play. Use an object pronoun in each sentence. Try to use an object pronoun as a direct object, as an indirect object, and as the object of a preposition.

_____

_____

_____

_____

_____

_____

_____

Tips for Your Own Writing: Proofreading..

Reread something that you have written. Identify all of the personal pronouns. Did you use *It's me*? Although that is often used in informal speech, remember that the correct written form is *It is I* because *I* is the subject, not the object. *I* follows a linking verb.

The object of this lesson is to get you to put object pronouns in the right form.

44 Usage: Double Negatives

One negative is enough! Avoid the double negative.

No, none, not, nobody, and *nothing* are negative words. Using two such negative words in the same sentence is called a *double negative.* Good writers avoid double negatives.

> **Incorrect:** I do **not** like **nothing** in my lunch box today.
> **Correct:**   I do **not** like anything in my lunch box today.

> **Incorrect:** You **can't** eat **no** lunch with us.
> **Correct:**   You **can't** eat any lunch with us.

The *n't* in *can't* stands for the negative word *not.* To avoid the double negative, watch for *not* in contractions such as *don't, won't, didn't,* and *isn't.*

The words *barely, hardly,* and *scarcely* are also used as negative words. Avoid using the negative word *not* with these words.

> **Incorrect:** I **couldn't hardly** eat after seeing that movie.
> **Correct:**   I could **hardly** eat after seeing that movie.

Show What You Know

Correct each double negative that is underlined below. Rewrite the words on the line.

1. Teresa <u>couldn't do nothing</u> with her clay. _____

2. She <u>hadn't barely</u> started sculpting class. _____

3. Todd <u>didn't have no</u> clay on his table. _____

4. He <u>wasn't hardly</u> ready to get his hands dirty. _____

5. The teacher thought he <u>wouldn't never</u> get Todd to try. _____

6. In fact, Todd <u>wouldn't have none</u> of it. _____

Score: _____   Total Possible: 6

Proofread

The writer of the following report has overlooked four double negatives. Draw a delete mark through each mistake and write the correction above it.

Example: I don't want ~~none~~. (any)

A true recycler, the hermit crab doesn't believe in no waste. Because it doesn't have no protective covering for its soft stomach, it goes looking for one. It can't hardly wait to find an old shell. A cast-off shell from a shellfish such as a conch will do just fine. The crab pulls itself into its adopted "home." It uses tail hooks to hold the shell in place and guards the opening with crusher claws. Once it is inside, nobody won't bother Mr. or Ms. Hermit Crab!

Practice

Imagine that you are writing a TV ad for a lunch food, such as the one in the picture. Write a description, or write a dialogue between two lunch items, such as a banana and a cookie. Avoid using double negatives.

_____

_____

_____

_____

_____

_____

_____

_____

_____

Tips for Your Own Writing: Proofreading..................................

Select a piece of your own writing. Read aloud any sentences that contain negative words. Do you hear more than one negative word in any of these sentences? Watch particularly for contractions that contain the *n't*.

 *R*emember to use only one negative word in a sentence.

45 Review: Pronoun Agreement and Double Negatives

A. In the following article, underline the seven subject pronouns.

Maria Mitchell, the daughter of a sea captain in Nantucket, Massachusetts, lived in the 1800s. Maria helped in her father's business. He adjusted navigation instruments for oceangoing ships. They needed to be very accurate instruments. In the meantime, Maria developed an interest in astronomy. She learned how to use a telescope and studied books on astronomy in her free time.

Through careful study and observation, Maria became a very fine astronomer. On October 1, 1847, she noticed a hazy object in the sky. It was an unknown comet. Maria was the first to see it. A famous discoverer was she. Honors came to her, including a medal from the king of Denmark. Later she became professor of astronomy at Vassar College.

Score: _____   Total Possible: 7

B. In each sentence below, identify one object pronoun. If the pronoun is a direct object, draw one line under it. Draw two lines under a pronoun that is an indirect object, and circle a pronoun that is the object of a preposition.

Living things develop defenses against other living things that might eat them. Some plants use poison against their enemies to give them a nasty surprise. If you like the outdoors, poison ivy may be quite familiar to you. Oil from this plant irritates human skin, causing eruptions on it. Eating monkshood, a common garden plant, would probably kill you. But, in fact, poisonous plants can be very useful to us, too. Rotenone, from a tropical plant, weakens harmful insects or kills them. Rotenone breaks down quickly in the environment and doesn't harm it. The garden plant foxglove yields a drug, digitalis. Doctors give it to heart patients.

Score: _____   Total Possible: 9

C. Underline five sentences with double negatives that you find in this article. Write those sentences correctly on the lines.

In 1974 a discovery was made near Xi'an (Sian) in China. This wasn't no ordinary find. Buried at the tomb of China's first emperor was a life-size army of 7,500 soldiers and horses made of terra cotta, a type of pottery. Hardly any of them weren't broken.

Archaeologists couldn't hardly believe their good luck. (An archaeologist is a scientist who studies objects from past cultures.) The creators of this "army" didn't want no one to disturb the tomb. Some figures were "booby-trapped." For example, moving a particular object may set off the release of a spear or arrow.

Would you like to see the terra-cotta army? If you think you won't never have the chance, you may be wrong. The Chinese government is allowing some of the figures to be displayed outside of China.

_____

_____

_____

_____

_____

_____

_____

Score: _____   Total Possible: 5

REVIEW SCORE: _____   REVIEW TOTAL: 21

46 Grammar: Nouns

How could we speak or write without the ability to name things? Nouns are essential.

························· Did You Know? ·····························

A **noun** is a word that tells who or what did the action or was acted upon by the verb in the sentence.

Concrete nouns name things that you can see or touch. They can fit in the blank in this sentence: The _____ stood there.

> house   star   ice   cloth   horse   woman   child

Abstract nouns name intangible ideas or qualities—things that cannot be seen or touched.

> fairness   danger   truth   fear   love   courage   faith

A **common noun** is the general name for someone or something. A **proper noun** is the name of a particular person or place. It may consist of more than one word and begin with capital letters, except for small words such as *of*.

Common Nouns	Proper Nouns
city	Philadelphia
document	Declaration of Independence
author	Thomas Jefferson

Show What You Know

Write *C* or *P* above each underlined noun, identifying it as either a common or a proper noun. Circle any proper noun that is not capitalized.

We expect earthquakes to strike <u>areas</u> along the edges of continental plates. But one of
1

the strongest <u>earthquakes</u> in <u>North America</u> struck along the <u>mississippi river</u> in 1811. This is
2   **3**   **4**

right in the center of the North American plate. During and after the quake, one steamboat

<u>captain</u> observed that the <u>river</u> reversed its course and ran backward. An observer in <u>kentucky</u>
5   **6**   **7**

reported that "the ground waved like a <u>field</u> of corn before the breeze." In northwestern
                                        8

Tennessee, twenty square miles of woodland sank. We know this place today as <u>Reelfoot Lake</u>.
                                                                                9

Score: _____   Total Possible: 11

Practice

The paragraph below is missing all of its nouns. First, read the paragraph and then choose the nouns you wish to add in the blanks. Your paragraph may be serious or humorous.

_____ is the worst _____ of the
    1   2

_____. This unnecessary and irritating _____ is
    3   4

produced when _____ is changed electronically. The first
                    5

_____ was made by mixing _____ such as _____
    6   7   8

and _____. The _____ is horrible. I think I like
       9   10

_____ better!
    11

Revise

Read the paragraph below. Above each underlined noun, write another noun that is more specific and interesting.

The average bee group has one important lady, several hundred males, and thousands of
                  1   2

young females called workers. By studying these workers, people have found that bees are
                                                          3

smart, complex, and highly social things.
                                4

Worker bees have many things to do. They clean and protect the home. They also look for
                              5   6

juice to make honey.
 7

Tips for Your Own Writing: Revising...

Review a piece of your writing. Look at the nouns and check to see that you chose the most specific and interesting noun you could in each case. Remember, precise word choice is an important part of effective writing.

 Common nouns or proper nouns?—it's a capital difference.

47 Grammar: Pronouns

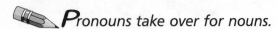 *Pronouns take over for nouns.*

······················· **Did You Know?**·······························

A <u>pronoun</u> is a word that takes the place of a noun or another pronoun. It keeps language from becoming repetitive.

> **Without Pronouns:** **Heinz** wanted to make **Heinz's** best shot.
> **With Pronouns:** **Heinz** wanted to make **his** best shot.

Pronouns can be in the first, the second, or the third person.

First person refers to the person(s) speaking.

Subject	Possessive	Object
I, we	my, our	me, us

Second person refers to the person(s) being spoken to.

Subject	Possessive	Object
you	your	you

Third person refers to a person, animal, or thing being spoken of.

Subject	Possessive	Object
he, she	his, her	him, her
it	its	it
they	their	them

The pronouns *it* and *its* refer to animals or things, never to people.

Show What You Know

Above each underlined pronoun, write *1*, *2*, or *3* for first, second, or third person.

I think that Wolfgang A. Mozart was one of the greatest composers who ever lived. <u>He</u>
₁   ₂

wrote an astounding number of great musical works. Opera fans especially love Mozart's

operas. One of the best of <u>them</u> is *The Marriage of Figaro*. In this opera, a woman tries to
₃

regain <u>her</u> husband's affection. But Mozart's music is what makes this opera special. <u>It</u> is simply
₄   ₅

sublime! Mozart composed orchestra and piano pieces, too. Have <u>you</u> ever listened to any of
₆

<u>his</u> pieces?
₇

Score: _____   **Total Possible: 7**

Proofread

Mike's story about last night's storm contains five noun repetitions that could be improved by using a pronoun. Two articles will also need to be deleted. Use the proper proofreading mark to delete each repeated noun and the two articles.

Example: Sarah rode ~~Sarah's~~ her bike.

Hiss! Crash! Boom! So began last night's terrible thunderstorm. At about eight o'clock,

Dad was finishing up his gardening. Dad came running in the house and cried, "This is going

to be a big one. Put the awnings down and fasten the awnings. Awnings are especially prone

to wind damage."

We heard three very loud claps of thunder in a row. On the fourth, the oak tree shuddered

and split. The oak tree crashed to the ground. At about that time, we smelled

ozone, a pungent chemical. Mom knew what this odor was, because

Mom's major in college was meteorology, the study of weather.

Practice

Write four descriptive sentences about a person you know well. You can write about a friend, parent, grandparent, or anyone you're close to. Use at least four pronouns to refer to that person. Avoid repeating nouns awkwardly.

_____

_____

_____

_____

_____

_____

Tips for Your Own Writing: Proofreading................................

Pronouns have gender. *Masculine gender* refers to male people (*he, him, his*). *Feminine gender* refers to female people (*she, her, hers*). *Neuter gender* refers to animals or things (*it, its*). Find the pronouns in a piece of your writing. Did you use the appropriate form for each gender?

*B*e pro-pronoun. Use pronouns where they improve your writing.

48 Grammar: Verbs

Verbs are the threads that tie language together. How could we speak or write without expressing actions or states of being?

·····················Did You Know?·····················

A <u>verb</u> tells what the person, place, or thing in a sentence is doing, or it <u>links</u> or connects the subject to the rest of the sentence. A verb might tell about being rather than acting.

Many verbs are *action verbs*.

> Hurricane gusts **whipped** the boat.
> The mast of the ship **crashed** to the deck.

Linking verbs express the existence of something or link the subject with a word that renames or modifies it.

> Here **is** a weather chart.　　(*expresses a state of being*)
> The storm **becomes** a hurricane.　(*links the subject to the renaming word*)

Linking Verbs

am	was	become	look	smell
is	were	feel	remain	sound
are	appear	grow	seem	taste

Some verbs can be used either as action verbs or as linking verbs.

> Rena **feels** the wet grass on her bare feet.　(*action verb*)
> After walking in the grass, Rena **feels** good.　(*linking verb*)

Show What You Know

Underline the verb in each sentence. Then circle each verb that is a linking verb.

Last year, we visited Uncle Taylor's turkey farm. It is quite modern. The birds dwell in climate-controlled buildings rather than outdoors. The turkeys' claws hardly ever touch the ground. I imagined majestic, colorful, flying birds. But these turkeys appear dull. Only plain, white feathers cover them. Moreover, the turkeys seem quite stupid. Nevertheless, they taste good at the Thanksgiving feast!

Score: _____　　Total Possible: 13

Practice

Think about a ride you have enjoyed in an amusement park—a roller coaster, for example. Think of strong action verbs you might use to describe the ride or to express your emotions while on the ride. Write two sentences about the ride, using action verbs.

1. _____

_____

_____

2. _____

_____

_____

Now think of some linking verbs from this lesson that you might use to convey information about the ride. Write two sentences about the ride, using some of these verbs.

1. _____

_____

2. _____

_____

Revise

Read the paragraph below. Above each underlined verb, write another verb that is stronger and more interesting.

The Activity Club at Geller School met in September to <u>get</u> a name for our new
₁

newspaper. Vance Vedder <u>said</u>, "The Activity Club Journal." Sandra Yee <u>said</u>, "The News and
₂   ₃

Doers." The club members <u>talked</u> for two hours. We voted three times, and each time the vote
₄

was 4–4. Then Beth Gonzalez <u>said</u>, "The Geller Gazette." On the fourth vote, this name
₅

<u>was picked</u>.
₆

Tips for Your Own Writing: Revising ....

Select a piece of your own writing. Identify the action verbs that you used. Then, ask yourself, "Are any of these action verbs too vague? Could they be replaced with stronger, clearer action verbs?" Think of other verbs you could use. A thesaurus may help you.

 With effort and practice, you can put more verve in your verbs.

49 Grammar: Irregular Verbs

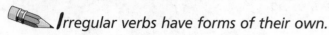*Irregular verbs have forms of their own.*

·····························Did You Know?·····························

Most English verbs are regular. Regular verbs add *-ed* to form the past tense. The past participle is formed in the same way, but it also uses a helping word such as *is*, *was*, *have*, or *had*.

> *Present*—I **walk** a lot.   *Past Tense*—I **walked** yesterday.
> *Past Participle*—I **have walked** every day.

Verbs that do not form the past and past participle by adding *-ed* are irregular verbs.

> *Present*—I **sing** a lot.   *Past Tense*—I **sang** yesterday.
> *Past Participle*—I **have sung** every day.

Present Tense	Past Tense	Past Participle	Present Tense	Past Tense	Past Participle (+ helping verb)
catch	caught	caught	make	made	made
do	did	done	ring	rang	rung
eat	ate	eaten	run	ran	run
fall	fell	fallen	speak	spoke	spoken
freeze	froze	frozen	take	took	taken
give	gave	given	teach	taught	taught
go	went	gone	throw	threw	thrown
grow	grew	grown	win	won	won

Show What You Know

Write the correct past tense form of the verb in parentheses to complete each sentence.

Beverly Sills _____ up in New York City. From the time she was very young, she wanted to
    1(grow)

become an opera singer. She _____ her operatic career in 1946. Then she joined the New
                            2(begin)

York City Opera in 1955. She _____ one of the greatest operatic sopranos of the mid-
                            3(become)

1900s. She _____ fame for her versatile voice and rich tones. Her superior abilities and warm
          4(win)

personality _____ her popular with audiences and musicians.
            5(make)

Score: _____   Total Possible: 5

Practice

The paragraph below is missing its verbs. In each blank, write a verb that makes sense in the sentence.

Opera is a play in which the characters _____ their

1

lines. It is not a drama where the characters _____

their lines. Opera singers must _____ fancy costumes

2

and _____ their roles. They may also have to

3   4

_____ several languages and _____ to

5

other countries to study.

6

Revise

Read the paragraph below. Above the underlined words, write verbs that make sense in the story and are in the correct form.

Enrico Caruso <u>got to be</u> a famous opera singer. He first <u>singed</u> at Naples in 1894. Then he

1   2

<u>gone</u> to London to perform at Covent Garden. In 1903, he <u>sanged</u> at the Metropolitan Opera

3   4

in New York City. He had a very powerful voice. His notes <u>rung</u> across the stage and thrilled

5

audiences. He <u>becomed</u> one of the most famous opera stars in history.

6

Tips for Your Own Writing: Revising ....

Review a piece of your writing. Check the verb forms. Use these clues to see that you have used the correct forms of the verbs. Find verbs you have used and put each verb into one of these frames.

Today I _____.   Yesterday I _____.   Tomorrow I will _____.

A dictionary can be your best friend when you need to check the forms of irregular verbs.

50 Grammar: Adjectives

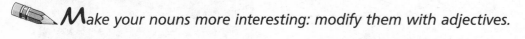 *Make your nouns more interesting: modify them with adjectives.*

Did You Know?

An adjective is a word that modifies a noun. *Modifies* **means "describes" or "gives additional information about something."**

Some adjectives tell *what kind.*

> Jamael's sister is a **brilliant** painter.

Some adjectives tell *how many.*

> The band played **many** marches for the crowd.

Some adjectives tell *which one.*

> I liked the **third** song.

Articles (*the, a, an***) are a special type of adjective, also called determiners because they signal that a noun follows.**

> **The** tune is **an** old favorite.

Adjectives come before the words they modify or after a linking verb.

> The **shiny** horn blared. The drummer seems **sleepy.**

A **proper adjective** **is formed from a proper noun. It is always capitalized.**

> The **Italian** language is used in musical notation.

Show What You Know

Underline the adjectives (including articles) in the sentences below. Circle any proper adjectives that should be capitalized.

1. An oceanographer studies many aspects of the seas and oceans.

2. On Earth, the oceans are vast, deep pools of water.

3. But the water in oceans and seas is not drinkable.

4. It contains enormous amounts of common table salt.

5. The Pacific Ocean is the largest ocean on Earth.

6. It has many powerful currents, including the brazil Current.

Score: _____   Total Possible: 19

Practice

Think of a place you like to visit—perhaps the seashore, the lake, or the desert. Close your eyes and picture the place, or a part of it. Think of six adjectives to describe it. The adjectives can describe any aspect of your mental picture—sight, sound, smell, or touch. Write the adjectives on the lines.

_____

_____

_____

_____

_____

Now think of three adjectives that describe your *feelings* about this place. You can use the sentence form "I feel . . ." to express these feelings. Write the sentence on the lines.

_____

_____

_____

Revise

Revise the paragraph below by adding at least seven adjectives to give more details and make the picture clearer and more interesting to the reader. Write the adjectives above the nouns they modify.

The sun shone on the beach and warmed the sand. Waves splashed back and forth across the cove. Light sparkled on the waves. A boat sailed past in the distance. With a snort, a scuba diver rose suddenly to the surface by the pier. People played a game of volleyball at one end of the beach while children made sand castles at the other end. The sights, sounds, and smells of the beach made it the place to be.

Tips for Your Own Writing: Revising ....

Choose a piece that you have written. Identify the adjectives that you used. Did you use adjectives like *good, bad,* or *nice* when you might have used a more descriptive adjective? Replace any adjectives that do not give enough detail.

*A*djectives help people see the world as a colorful, interesting place.

101

51 Grammar: Articles

*K*now *your articles:* the, an, *and* a.

....................................**Did You Know?**..................................

Articles are special adjectives that are used only with nouns. They are also called determiners because they signal that a noun follows.

The definite article *the* is used with a noun when the noun refers to a particular thing.

>   **The** Olympic swimmer now speaks at schools.

The indefinite articles *a* and *an* are used with a noun when the noun refers to no particular thing.

>   We heard **a** swimmer speak about careers in sports.
>   Next week **an** acrobat will talk to us.

The article *a* is used before a word that begins with a consonant sound: *a* speech.

The article *an* is used before a word that begins with a vowel sound: *an* audience.

Show What You Know

Fill in each blank with the appropriate article: *the, an,* or *a.*

   Jacques Cousteau was _____ important ocean explorer of this century. He made

1

many contributions to oceanography, _____ science of oceans. Cousteau developed

2

oxygen tanks for diving. Before divers had these tanks, they had to wear very heavy, awkward

suits. Cousteau's contribution was, therefore, _____ very important one. Cousteau studied

3

ocean plants and animals that are almost unknown. He also explored shipwrecks. One of

Cousteau's major concerns was pollution. He opposed _____ French government for

4

dumping nuclear wastes at sea.

   It is not _____ exaggeration to say that Jacques Cousteau popularized oceanography.

5

His TV specials made millions more aware of _____ earth's oceans.

6

Score: _____   Total Possible: 6

Proofread

Gerry's report on whale music has six mistakes in its use of articles. Use the proper proofreading mark to correct each mistake.

Example: I had ~~a~~ ^{an} apple for lunch.

Whales communicate by a astonishingly rich language. They often use a area of the deep sea called the sound channel to send their sound messages over very long distances. We're not sure what all the whale sounds mean. But whales are known to respond to calls for help from an great distance. Scientists wonder whether the sounds are produced on a hourly or daily schedule of some kind.

In fact, whales seem to produce two distinct groups of sounds. One group includes low-pitched barks, whistles, screams, and moans that humans can hear. Whales also make another group of sounds at an high frequency, or pitch, which humans cannot hear. Whales may use these clicks or squeaks like an kind of radar. Perhaps they locate prey or orient themselves using these sounds.

Practice

Look at the picture. Write three sentences to describe what is happening. Try to use the articles *the* and *a* at least one time each.

1. _____

_____

2. _____

_____

3. _____

_____

Tips for Your Own Writing: Proofreading...

Choose a piece of your own writing. To check that you used the appropriate article with each noun, read your writing aloud. Listening to the beginning sound of each noun will help you know whether you chose the right article.

 What an *article! You needed* the *articles* a, an, *and the to complete* the *lessons.*

Lesson

52 Grammar: Adverbs

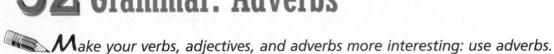 *Make your verbs, adjectives, and adverbs more interesting: use adverbs.*

······························**Did You Know?**·····························

An adverb is a word that modifies a verb, an adjective, or another adverb. We form many adverbs by adding *-ly* **to an adjective. We often change a final** *y* **to** *i* **before adding the** *-ly***.**

quick + -ly = quickly
happy + -ly = happily

When adverbs are used with verbs, they tell *how, when, where,* **or** *to what extent***.**

Brae walked **hurriedly** to the mailbox.
She slammed the door **afterward.**
Then she stomped **upstairs.**
Now Brae relaxed **completely.**

Adverbs that tell *to what extent* **can also modify adjectives and other adverbs.**

Arturo's house was **almost** invisible.
But now the fog is lifting **very** rapidly.

Show What You Know

Underline each adverb in the article. Draw a line to the word that each adverb modifies.

Listen carefully. You can play a violin correctly. First, hold the instrument securely against the neck and under the chin. Take the bow firmly in the free hand. Apply the bow to the strings so that it barely touches them. Then pull the bow evenly. Do this without breaking contact with the strings. When you very nearly reach the end of the arc, reverse the direction of the bow. Now you push it. The sound you hear may be rather scratchy. But remember, learning to play the violin means practicing regularly.

Score: _____   Total Possible: 22

104

Practice

Write an adverb in each blank in the paragraph. Choose adverbs that tell about the actions of marching bands.

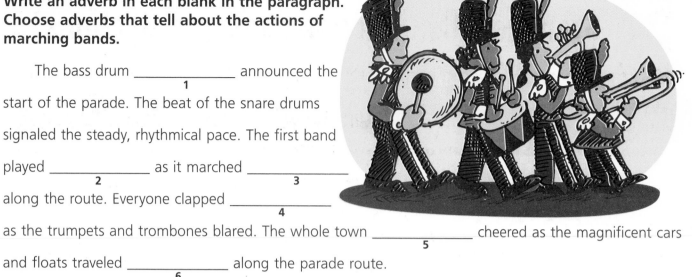

The bass drum _____ announced the
                    1

start of the parade. The beat of the snare drums

signaled the steady, rhythmical pace. The first band

played _____ as it marched _____
          2   **3**

along the route. Everyone clapped _____
                                          4

as the trumpets and trombones blared. The whole town _____ cheered as the magnificent cars
                                                             5

and floats traveled _____ along the parade route.
                           6

Revise

Revise the paragraph below by adding at least four adverbs to give more details and make the picture clearer and more interesting to the reader. Insert carets to show where the adverbs should be added.

Example: Beat the drum.
         slowly
         ^

Create your own orchestra. Find some empty pop bottles. Fill them with

water at different levels. To "play" them, blow across their tops. Take a jar with a lid. Put some

dried beans in the jar and close the lid. Shake the jar to make a rhythmic sound. Find some old

metal pots and pans and a clean paintbrush. Invert the pans and "play" them with the brush,

like a snare drum. If you want to get fancy, make your own set of wind chimes. Use sticks,

string, and small pieces of metal for the "chimes." You can make your own music.

Tips for Your Own Writing: Proofreading

Select something from your own writing and find the adverbs. Be sure that you did not use too many adverbs in any one place, as in this sentence: *I read a very, extremely, unbelievably long book.* Like adjectives, adverbs should be used with restraint.

Here is very useful advice: write quite descriptively with adverbs.

53 Grammar: Conjunctions and Interjections

Use conjunctions to connect words or word groups. Use interjections to express emotion.

Did You Know?

A **conjunction** is a word that connects words or groups of words.

Coordinating conjunctions such as *and, but,* and *or* connect related words, groups of words, or sentences.

> Meiko **and** Bob go to dance class together.
> The recital was entertaining **but** long.
> Bob danced in the first dance **and** in the finale.
> Meiko forgot the step, **or** her foot slipped.

Correlative conjunctions are conjunctions used in pairs to connect sentence parts.

> **Neither** Tessa **nor** Kato wanted to be first in the lineup.
> Trini had to decide **whether** to dance **or** to study piano.
> We saw **both** Sharon **and** Quinn in the jazz dance.

An **interjection** is a word or words that express emotion.

> **Wow!** Your performance in the dance recital was stupendous.
> **Oh,** I want to learn how to dance.

Use either an exclamation point or a comma after an interjection. If the emotion being expressed is strong, use the exclamation point.

Show What You Know

Circle each conjunction and underline each interjection in the paragraph below.

Suddenly I heard, "Yipe! It's a big *snake*." The poor snake simply wanted peace and quiet.

It neither rattled nor hissed. It quietly uncoiled, and then it slithered away. I wanted to follow

the snake, but Terri told me to stay away from it. "Look out!" she said. "It's gone under that

rock." Both Dr. Herkimer and I are snake scientists. Oh, and we are both afraid of snakes!

Score: _____   **Total Possible: 11**

Practice

Look at the picture of a dog show. Write three sentences that describe the scene. Use conjunctions in at least two of the sentences, perhaps to compare and contrast the owners and their dogs. (Name them if you would like.)

1. _____

_____

_____

2. _____

_____

_____

3. _____

_____

_____

Revise

Revise the paragraphs below by adding at least four conjunctions and one interjection to improve the writing. Use proper proofreading marks.

Example: We called her. We waited for her.
(and inserted)

Susan ran home from school. She was very excited. She raced in the front door. She

looked for her parents. As soon as she saw her father, she yelled, "I won."

"Calm down," said Mr. Campbell. "Tell us what you won."

Susan reported that she had won first place in the science fair. She had gotten a trophy.

She had gotten a medal.

Mrs. Campbell congratulated Susan. She hugged Susan. Mrs. Campbell cried. She did not

cry long. Mr. Campbell smiled a lot. He told Susan they were very proud of her.

Tips for Your Own Writing: Revising..

Choose a piece of your own writing. Did you use any interjections? If so, did you use them only occasionally? Using too many interjections is like the boy who cried "Wolf!" too often. After a while, the excitement wears off. Save interjections for special occasions.

 Wow! Conjunctions and interjections in the same lesson.

54 Grammar: Prepositions

 Use prepositional phrases to modify words in sentences.

Did You Know?

A **preposition** connects a noun or pronoun to the rest of the sentence. The noun or pronoun that follows the preposition is called the **object of the preposition.**

The object, along with the preposition, its object, and any words that modify the object, make up a *prepositional phrase.* This phrase gives more information about the sentence.

> We glanced **across** *the treacherous river.*

A prepositional phrase modifies a noun, pronoun, verb, adjective, or adverb. In the first sentence, the prepositional phrase *along the beach* is an *adverb phrase* that modifies the verb *walked.* In the second sentence, the prepositional phrase *along the beach* is an *adjective phrase* that modifies the noun *walk.*

> We walked *along the beach.*
> Our walk *along the beach* was enjoyable.

Prepositions

about	before	down	of	to
above	behind	for	on	under
across	below	from	over	up
after	beneath	in	since	with
against	beside	like	through	without

Show What You Know

Underline each prepositional phrase. Circle the preposition.

Sweat was running down Matt's face. He couldn't believe that his opponent Marvin would

clobber him, even though Marvin *was* champion of the school district. "Fifteen-love. Thirty-

love." The scores were announced over the speaker! Matt tried to remember all he'd been

taught: grip the end of the racket, but not too tightly. Stay limber and don't stand in one spot.

Keep eyes on the ball. Now a serve was coming across the net. Matt crossed his fingers.

Score: _____   **Total Possible: 14**

Practice

Think of the sights, sounds, feelings, and smells of a storm. It could be a snowstorm, thunderstorm, or hurricane. Write a sentence or poem using as many prepositional phrases as you can.

Example: Rain *from the dark clouds in the sky* pounded *on the roof of the house* and pelted the trees *in the yard* as the lightning flashed *across the sky.*

Possible beginnings:

　　Over the trees in the yard

　　In the dark of night

_____

_____

_____

_____

_____

_____

_____

_____

Revise

Revise the paragraph below by adding at least four prepositional phrases to provide details about the heat, the drought, or the rainy season. Use proper proofreading marks.

　　　　In the evening,　under the beautiful elm tree
Example: We sat outside.

　　Hot, dry winds sweep across much of southern Asia. The sun bakes the earth, and crops

cannot grow. The people wait for the rainy season. The coming of the rain means that they

can plant crops and produce food.

Tips for Your Own Writing: Revising..

Choose a piece that you have written recently. Look for places to add prepositional phrases to provide additional information or add interesting details to your sentences. Always try to place each phrase next to the word it modifies.

 Prepositions add details to your writing.

Lesson

55 Review: Parts of Speech

A. **Underline the four proper nouns in the article below.**

Lucille Ball was one of the most successful comedians of all time. She and her husband,

Desi Arnaz, created an incredibly popular TV show in the 1950s. It featured their New York

apartment and best friend, "Ethel Mertz."

Score: _____   Total Possible: 4

B. **Write a pronoun from the list that best completes each sentence.**

you   her   them   we

1. Marla twisted _____ ankle on the ice yesterday.

2. Ben and Rae have won the skating match. Let's congratulate _____.

3. Can _____ join our teams together to put on a bigger skating show?

4. "I know _____ will like skating as much as I do," said the champ to her son.

Score: _____   Total Possible: 4

C. **Above each underlined verb, write *A* if it is an action verb and *L* if it is a linking verb.**

1. Beavers build lodges in artificial lakes.

2. A lodge is a mound of sticks with an interior chamber.

3. As for the artificial lake, the beaver creates that by damming a stream.

4. It seems strange that a beaver can make such a difference.

Score: _____   Total Possible: 5

D. **Underline fourteen adjectives (including articles) in the report below. Circle one proper adjective.**

Pluto is the last planet revolving around the sun. It was discovered in 1930 by American

astronomer Clyde Tombaugh. Before this important discovery, astronomers suspected the

existence of a ninth planet. They had noticed that a force seemed to pull the seventh planet,

Uranus, and the eighth planet, Neptune, off their orbits.

Score: _____   Total Possible: 15

E. Fill in each blank with the appropriate article: *the*, *an*, or *a*.

1. Find _____ player to pluck the banjo.

2. If you play the harp, then find _____ orchestra to play in.

3. This is _____ guitar that I played in the concert last year.

Score: _____   Total Possible: 3

F. Underline the adverb in each of the three sentences below.

1. Charles Dickens wrote often about children's hardships.

2. Mrs. Havisham trains Estella to treat all men cruelly.

3. Do you know this story well? It is Dickens's *Great Expectations*.

Score: _____   Total Possible: 3

G. Underline eight conjunctions and circle two interjections.

Have you ever experienced a partial or total eclipse of the sun? Oh, my! It's an exciting experience. The moon passes between the sun and Earth. It casts a shadow on Earth. Not only does the sky darken, but also the air chills. Wow, it feels just like nightfall! Both before and after the deepest part of the eclipse, you have to be careful not to look directly at the sun. To do so could injure your eyes. Whether the eclipse is total or partial, a solar eclipse is something to remember.

Score: _____   Total Possible: 10

H. Underline five prepositional phrases below. Above the phrase, write the part of speech that it modifies (noun, verb, adjective).

1. Bread is a staple food for many people.

2. Much of the flour used to make bread comes from wheat.

3. The wheat heads on the stalk tip provide flour's raw material.

4. To harvest wheat, machines beat the heads against a hard surface.

5. The grain is then milled into flour.

Score: _____   Total Possible: 10

REVIEW SCORE: _____   REVIEW TOTAL: 54

56 Grammar: Combining Sentences I

You can form compound sentences in more than one way.

Did You Know?

Using compounds to combine short sentences can lead to smoother, less choppy writing.

When sentences have the same subject and verb, you can combine them easily.

> Darryl eats apples.   Darryl eats plums.
> Darryl eats **apples and plums.**

When two sentences have the same subject but different verbs and objects, they can also be combined.

> Heather plays soccer.   Heather writes poetry.
> Heather **plays soccer and writes poetry.**

Sentences with the same verb and object but different subjects can also be combined. Many times the form of the verb will change when it becomes plural.

> Diehl goes to summer camp.   Timothy goes to summer camp.
> **Diehl and Timothy** go to summer camp.

If *I* is one subject in a compound subject, it always comes *last.*

> **Timothy and I** go to summer camp.

Show What You Know

Combine each pair of sentences into one compound sentence.

1. England is in the British Isles. Scotland is in the British Isles.

_____

2. Aunt Tillie visited England. Aunt Tillie visited Scotland.

_____

3. She climbed mountains in Scotland. She visited gardens in England.

_____

4. Tillie sipped tea in the afternoon. Tillie ate scones in the afternoon.

_____

Score: _____   Total Possible: 4

Practice

Make a personal profile. First, list four of your physical characteristics such as hairstyle or color, height, and eye color. Next, list four foods that you like. Finally, list four things that you like to do for fun.

Physical Characteristics

_____   _____

_____   _____

Favorite Foods

_____   _____

_____   _____

Things I Like to Do

_____   _____

_____   _____

Using the information above, write two compound sentences telling about yourself.

1. _____

_____

2. _____

_____

Revise

Revise the paragraph below by rewriting at least two sentences as compound sentences. Use proper proofreading marks.

Example: Cats ⋀ are mammals. ~~Dogs are mammals too.~~
    and dogs

Alligators belong to the family *Crocodylidae.* Crocodiles belong to that family, too. They

look a lot alike. Some of the crocodiles' bottom teeth show when they close their mouths.

Alligators' teeth are hidden when they close their mouths. Also, crocodiles have narrow

snouts. Alligators have broad snouts.

Tips for Your Own Writing: Revising..

Choose a piece of your own writing. Look for short, choppy sentences and see whether combining them will improve your writing. Also, look for sentences that are too long. Sometimes a very long sentence should be divided into two shorter sentences.

*B*e a joiner! Combine sentences whenever appropriate.

57 Grammar: Combining Sentences II

Do two sentences have some words in common? You may be able to combine the sentences by using an appositive.

.... **Did You Know?**.................................

Sometimes we can combine two sentences by taking information from one sentence and attaching it to a closely related noun or a phrase in another sentence. Information that is "attached" in this way is called an *appositive.* If it is at the beginning or end of a sentence, you need only one comma after it or before it.

> A river always has a mouth. A mouth is the place where it flows into a larger body of water.
> A river always has a mouth, **the place where it flows into a larger body of water.**

When an appositive adds information but is not necessary to establish the meaning of the sentence, set it off with commas. Delete the appositive and see whether the sentence has the same meaning.

> Our swimming coach teaches summer school. Mrs. Santos is our swimming coach.
> Mrs. Santos, **our swimming coach,** teaches summer school.

When an appositive is needed to clarify something, do *not* use commas.

> Rube and Lou played baseball tonight. Rube and Lou are Hornets team members.
> Hornets team members **Rube and Lou** played baseball tonight.

Show What You Know

Use an appositive to combine each pair of sentences below.

1. Every country has a capital. A capital is a city where government is run.

_____

2. Rome is full of ancient buildings. Rome is the capital of Italy.

_____

3. A small town is near Rome. The town has many ruins.

_____

Score: _____   Total Possible: 3

Practice

Look at the picture of a large public building. What adjectives does it bring to mind? Write four sentences with appositives about this building or a large public building in your own community (a local museum, for example). Include some descriptive details to help your reader visualize the building.

1. _____

   _____

2. _____

   _____

3. _____

   _____

4. _____

   _____

Revise

Revise the paragraph below. Use proper proofreading marks to combine at least two of the sentences by using appositives.

Example: High Street ∧our longest street∧ has a lot of trees. ~~It is our longest street~~.

New York City has more than seven and a half million people. It is the largest city in the

United States. It is one of the largest cities in the world. Only Tokyo, Japan, is larger. New York

is an important center for business, culture, and trade. It is also the home of the United

Nations. The city has banks, stock exchanges, and other financial institutions. These institutions

are located in the famous Wall Street area of the city. The Statue of Liberty is one of New

York's most well-known historic sites. It is visited by thousands of people every year.

Tips for Your Own Writing: Revising...

Select and reread a piece of your own writing. Are there any sentences you could combine by using an appositive? Combining information into one sentence will eliminate short, choppy sentences.

 When two sentences have a lot in common, they may want to join together.

58 Grammar: Combining Sentences III

Do two sentences have related ideas? Are they of equal importance? If the answer to these questions is yes, you may want to form compound sentences.

Did You Know?

Similar sentences can be combined when they have closely related ideas of equal importance. We can form such compound sentences by using the coordinating conjunctions *and, but,* or *or*. Place a comma after the first sentence and before the conjunction.

Use *and* to join sentences that have equal importance and similar ideas.

> Mr. Raeford will bake pies. Ms. Tasco will prepare salads.
> Mr. Raeford will bake pies, **and** Ms. Tasco will prepare salads.

Use *but* to join sentences that have equal importance and contrasting ideas.

> We had a picnic on Memorial Day. We stayed indoors on Independence Day.
> We had a picnic on Memorial Day, **but** we stayed indoors on Independence Day.

Use *or* to join sentences that have equal importance and that offer a choice.

> Play games with the children. Talk to the adults.
> Play games with the children, **or** talk to the adults.

Show What You Know

Use *and, but,* or *or* to form a compound sentence from each pair of sentences. Make sure you punctuate the sentences correctly.

1. We make homemade ice cream. Our neighbors enjoy sharing it with us.

_____

2. I like pistachio ice cream. My sister prefers strawberry ice cream.

_____

3. You can have homemade ice cream with us. You can go to the movie with them.

_____

Score: _____   Total Possible: 3

Practice

Think of holiday parties that your family has. Many families have celebrations at Thanksgiving or the Fourth of July. Use one of your family's special holiday celebrations in this writing assignment.

Write three sentences to describe the holiday celebration. Try to use each of the conjunctions *and, but,* and *or* at least one time.

1. _____

   _____

   _____

2. _____

   _____

3. _____

   _____

Revise

Revise the paragraph below by combining at least two sentences. Use proper proofreading marks to add the conjunctions *and, but,* and *or.*

Example: I like toppings on my ice cream. My brother doesn't.
                                      ^but

   Ice cream is made from milk products, sugar, and flavorings. It is a popular dairy treat. Ice

cream is eaten alone. It can also be eaten with cake or pie. It is the main ingredient in milk

shakes, sodas, and sundaes. The most popular flavor is vanilla. Chocolate is the next most

popular flavor. Ice cream can be found in many parts of the world. Americans eat more ice

cream than people in any other country.

Tips for Your Own Writing: Revising..

Select a piece of your own writing. Did you use the conjunctions *and, but,* and *or* to join sentences that have similar ideas? If the sentences do not have similar ideas, then you should not try to combine them.

When two sentences have a lot in common, they may belong together as one.

59 Grammar: Combining Sentences IV

When combining sentences, use any and all methods you can. Often, there is more than one good way to combine sentences.

Did You Know?

A big part of the writer's job is *selection*, that is, deciding which details to include (and which ones to leave out).

There is more than one way to combine the following sentences.

Mom just planted that rosebush.
The rosebush was full of blossoms.
We cut the rose.
The rose smelled very fragrant.
The rose had a bright red color.

We cut the bright red, fragrant rose from Mom's new rosebush, which was full of blossoms.

You could also write:

Planted recently by Mom, the rosebush yielded a bright red, fragrant rose, which we cut.

Show What You Know

Combine each set of sentences to create a new sentence. Write the new sentence on the line.

1. I recently read a new book.   Elbert Baze wrote it.
The book is *Dinosaur Music.*   It is an entertaining book.

_____

_____

2. I didn't know that the book signing was scheduled for Tuesday.
I made other plans with Bert and Ernie.

_____

_____

Score: _____   **Total Possible: 2**

Practice

At a book signing, an author greets people and signs copies of his or her latest book. Think about your favorite author. Imagine that you are going to this author's book signing. Write four sentences that you might say to the author.

1. _____

   _____

2. _____

   _____

3. _____

   _____

4. _____

   _____

Revise

Combine sentences in the paragraphs below using any of the methods you have learned. Use proper proofreading marks.

Example: I like to cook. Cooking takes time. My favorite recipe is spaghetti sauce.
(If I have time)

To make this pasta salad, you will need 1/2 lb of vermicelli. Vermicelli are very thin, long Italian noodles. Add 1/2 tsp. of salt to rapidly boiling water. Add the vermicelli to rapidly boiling water. Boil the vermicelli until tender. Drain them in a colander. Rinse them in cold water. Toss the noodles with a little oil. The noodles will stay separated.

Chop up 1/2 cup of black olives. Chop up 1/2 cup of green onions. Cut up 1/4 lb of provolone. Provolone is a mild Italian cheese. Mix the vermicelli, olives, onions, and cheese. Add mayonnaise. Add Italian dressing instead. Use salt, pepper, and garlic. Season the salad. Cover the salad. Refrigerate it for at least two hours.

Tips for Your Own Writing: Revising

Look at a piece of your own writing. Did you write many long sentences? Good writers use sentences of different lengths—both short and long—to add variety and interest to their writing.

 Don't be afraid of combining. Put those sentences together!

60 Review: Understanding and Combining Sentences

A. Choose a word or phrase from each column to build a sentence that makes sense. Using this method, make three sentences and write them on the lines.

Subject	Verb	Object	Preposition	Object
Benny	likes	the letters	in	her aunt
We	planted	sunshine	to	the clay pot
Courtney	mailed	a flower	for	the summer

1. _____

2. _____

3. _____

Score: _____   **Total Possible: 3**

B. Combine the sentences using *and*, *but*, or *or*. Write the sentences on the lines.

1. Oranges have vitamin C. Grapefruits have vitamin C.

_____

2. Go camping with Gene. Go to the movies with Leslie.

_____

3. We go to the movies frequently. We often see Leslie there.

_____

Score: _____   **Total Possible: 3**

C. Combine the following sentences, using an appositive. Write the sentence on the line.

Mrs. Tanaka is our librarian.   Mrs. Tanaka helps us with our research papers.

_____

Score: _____   **Total Possible: 1**

D. In each sentence, underline the subordinate clause and circle the main clause.

1. If you like my model ship, I'll make you one.

2. I think I can build it myself unless the kit is very complicated.

Score: _____   Total Possible: 4

E. Build a sentence using the provided sentence parts. Write the sentence on the line.

the green butterfly made a comeback   no one had seen in years   which

_____

Score: _____   Total Possible: 1

F. Combine the sentences using a participial phrase.

June was feeling sick.   June lay down and closed her eyes.

_____

Score: _____   Total Possible: 1

G. Combine the three sentences. Write the combined sentence on the line.

1. Berne is a new student.   **2.** He has red hair.   **3.** Berne is good at swimming.

_____

Score: _____ .   Total Possible: 1

H. Decide whether each sentence is a statement, question, exclamation, or request. Then write the correct punctuation on the line.

1. What time does Reeva get home from work this evening _____

2. Last night Janice got home at 8:30 _____

3. Don't stay out too late _____

Score: _____   Total Possible: 3

REVIEW SCORE: _____   REVIEW TOTAL: 17

121

Answer Key

---

1 Capitalization: Sentences, Titles, Days, Months, People

To capitalize or not to capitalize? Writers need to know how to answer this question about the words they write.

......................Did You Know?......................

The first word of a sentence is capitalized.

Please sign your name on the line at the bottom.

The names of people and pets are capitalized. So are people's initials and titles.

David Jacobson   Buck   Mr. Alfonso Garcia, Jr.

Words used to name relatives are capitalized *only* when the words are used as names or as part of names. They are not capitalized when preceded by a possessive pronoun, such as *my*, *your*, or *his*.

Will Dad pick up Mother at the train station?
I like staying with my grandmother.

The names of days, months, and holidays are capitalized, but the names of seasons are not.

On Monday, March 12, Sasha will interview the mayor.
Our family always has a picnic on Independence Day.

The pronoun *I* is capitalized.

Michael and I went to the video store.

Show What You Know

Circle the twenty-three letters that should be capitalized.

Galileo was an Italian astronomer and physicist. He was born in Italy on February 15, 1564. In 1609 Galileo built his first telescope. I heard about Galileo when I went to a planetarium with my father. The guide also talked about the Edwin P. Hubble Space Telescope, which was released on Monday, April 15, 1990. He spoke of the mission that made repairs on the telescope in 1993. Dr. Richard O. Covey and Dr. Kathryn C. Thornton were part of the crew that repaired the telescope.

Score: _____   Total Possible: 23

2

Proofread

Read the newspaper article. The writer left out 32 capital letters. Use the proper proofreading mark to show which letters should be capitalized.

Example: tuesday, april 5

Pet Party a Huge Success

On saturday, october 21, mr. and mrs. Howard C. jahn, jr., hosted an unusual event at their home to benefit a local animal shelter. they invited their friends to a costume party and competition—for their pets! Dozens of animals came to the party dressed as everything from donald duck to sherlock holmes. the jahns' dog, dodger, outfitted as count dracula, greeted the guests. First prize went to dr. caroline t. Sturgis's cockatoo, claude, for his Batman costume. "claude is very honored—i think," said Dr. sturgis. The jahns' nephew, mr. sidney K. abert, accompanied by his cat, delilah, said, "This is the best party that uncle Howard and aunt Stella have had since New year's eve."

Practice

Imagine that you have just met this girl and her dog. Write a short paragraph describing the meeting.

Review the paragraph to be sure that your child has:

• capitalized all names.

• capitalized the pronoun *I*.

• capitalized the first word of every sentence.

• written a paragraph that makes sense and relates to the topic

to the topic.

Tips for Your Own Writing: Proofreading..........................

Choose something you have written recently. Check your writing, asking yourself this question: Did I capitalize the first word in every sentence, all names, and the pronoun *I?*

Was the answer to the question "Yes"? Capital!

3

---

2 Capitalization: Places, Documents, Groups

Check the capitals—Declaration of Independence (document) for Americans (people) in Washington's White House (places).

......................Did You Know?......................

The names of specific places and things—cities, states, countries, divisions of the world, regions of the United States, streets, parks, and buildings—begin with a capital letter.

He flew from Boston, Massachusetts, to Paris, France.
The White House is located at 1600 Pennsylvania Avenue.

The names of historic documents begin with a capital letter.

The Magna Carta was written in 1215.

The names of races, nationalities, religions, and languages begin with a capital letter.

Many Cubans speak Spanish and English.

Show What You Know

Read the paragraph. On the lines, write the names that should have capital letters. Be sure to capitalize the words when you write them.

José Ubico was born in el salvador, a small country in central america. Ten years ago, he came to the united states, fleeing from the war in his homeland. José settled in los angeles where other salvadorans lived. José, who spoke spanish, learned english as well. One summer he went to washington, d. c., to see its many historic sights. His favorites were the jefferson memorial and the national archives museum where he saw copies of the constitution and the bill of rights.

1. El Salvador
2. Central America
3. United States
4. Los Angeles
5. Salvadorans
6. Spanish
7. English
8. Washington, D. C.
9. Jefferson Memorial
10. National Archives Museum
11. Constitution
12. Bill of Rights

Score: _____   Total Possible: 12

4

Proofread

Here is part of an essay about a world-famous building. The writer forgot to capitalize fifteen words. Use the proper proofreading mark to show which letters should be capitalized.

Example: south america

Every year, people from all over the world—americans, Japanese, british, chinese—come to see the taj mahal. It was built on the jumna River in agra, india, by Shah Jahan, the mogul emperor of India (1592–1666). The domed, white marble building is both an islamic monument and a tomb for the emperor's beloved queen, Mumtaz Mahal.

During his reign, Shah Jahan expanded india's territory in the far east. He also made islam the state religion and placed the country's capital in Delhi. But today he is remembered for constructing one of the world's most beautiful buildings—the Taj mahal.

Practice

Look at or imagine a map of your state. Choose a place that you think is interesting, unusual, or fun. Write a short paragraph telling about the place. Explain why a visitor to your state should plan to see this place.

Review the paragraph to be sure your child has:

• written about a place located in your state.

• given reasons why someone should visit the place.

• capitalized the names of specific places and things.

Tips for Your Own Writing: Proofreading..........................

Choose a piece of your own writing and give it to a partner to proofread while you proofread your partner's paper. Look for the names of places and things. Check to see whether your partner capitalized the names. Use proofreading marks to show what should be changed.

Remember ... a name always wears a cap! A capital letter, that is.

5

Lesson 3

Lesson

3 Capitalization: Titles

 Just as names of people are capitalized, names or titles of books and other materials are also capitalized.

......................................Did You Know?......................................

The first, last, and key words in the title of a book, magazine, movie, play, story, report, poem, painting, or song are capitalized.

The articles *a, an,* and *the*; the conjunctions *and, or, nor,* and *but*; and short prepositions such as *at, in,* and *of* are not capitalized unless they are the first or last words of the title. Notice that the titles of books, magazines, movies, and plays are italicized. When handwritten, these titles are underlined.

Jayne's favorite book is *A Wrinkle in Time.*
My mother likes to read the magazine *The New Yorker.*
Last night we watched the movie *Close Encounters of the Third Kind.*
A local theater group put on the play *A Raisin in the Sun.*
Henry read aloud the story "The Fox and the Crow."
The title of my report is "Lincoln as a Country Lawyer."
Tanya memorized the poem "Stopping by Woods on a Snowy Evening."
The painting "House by the Railroad" is by Edward Hopper.
The entire chorus joined in the song "Oh, What a Beautiful Morning!"

Show What You Know

Circle each word that should begin with a capital letter.

the kids' world almanac of baseball
sarah, plain and tall
under a telephone pole
raiders of the lost ark
nothing gold can stay

the little house on the prairie
tales and legends of india
ramona and the three wise persons
born on the fourth of july
song of the open road

Score: _____   Total Possible: 35

6

Proofread

Here is part of an article about how to write a report. The writer did not properly capitalize the nine titles in the article. Use the proper proofreading mark to show which letters should be capitalized.

Example: "the fall of the house of usher"

where to find information

After seeing the painting "a woman in Black at the opera," you have decided to write your report on the artist Mary Cassatt and call it "an american artist in Paris." You have some general information about Cassatt from encyclopedias, such as world book or Encyclopaedia britannica. Now, where else should you look? Read any books about the artist, such as an american impressionist or mary cassatt. Check the indexes of magazines, such as art and history and American artists, that might have articles about her.

Practice

What is your favorite book or movie? Write a short summary of the book or movie and then explain why you like it. Give your paragraph a title. Remember to underline the title of the book or movie in the summary.

_____

Review the paragraph to be sure your child has:

• written about a book or movie.

• summarized the book or movie.

• offered reasons why he or she liked the book or movie.

• written a title for the paragraph.

• capitalized the title of the book or movie correctly.

• capitalized the title of the paragraph correctly.

• underlined the title of the book or movie.

Tips for Your Own Writing: Proofreading.......................................

Look at several pieces of your own writing. Do they have titles? Did you use any titles within the copy? Check to see whether you capitalized the titles correctly.

Titles name books or other materials. Capitalize the key words in their names.

7

Lesson 4

Lesson

4 Capitalization: Direct Quotations

The first word of what I say is always capitalized. But if what I say is in parts, then it's a case of sometimes a capital and sometimes no capital.

......................................Did You Know?......................................

A direct quotation shows a person's words. A writer puts quotation marks before and after the quotation. The first word in the quotation is always capitalized.

"This award is a great honor," said Ms. Tannoy.
She exclaimed, "No one was more surprised than I was."

In a divided quotation, words such as *she said*, called speaker's tags, are in the middle of the quotation. The first word in the first part of the quotation is always capitalized. But the first word in the second part is capitalized *only* if it begins a new sentence.

"This award is a great honor," said Ms. Tannoy. "Thank you for giving it to me."
"This award," said Ms. Tannoy, "is a great honor."

Show What You Know

Read the sentences. Circle the twelve words that should begin with a capital letter.

Cara asked, "so what are we going to do our group report on?"

"i think," said Wayne, "we should do our report on the Squealing Wheels."

"oh, no," groaned Ahmed, "not that awful rock group again!"

"the Wheels are great," Wayne insisted. "they've had three number-one hits."

"let's vote," Cara interrupted. "all those for the Squealing Wheels? All those against? Okay, no Wheels. Any other suggestions?"

"if we want to do a music topic," Rachel offered, "how about focusing on a particular trend, like the return to acoustic performances?"

"that's a good idea," said Cara. "what do you guys think?"

"it's okay, with me," said Ahmed, "if it's okay, with Wayne."

Wayne grumbled, "yeah, all right. But I still say the Wheels are the best."

Score: _____   Total Possible: 12

8

Proofread

Here are some famous quotations. They are missing six capital letters. Use the proper proofreading mark to show which letters should be capitalized.

Example: Eleanor Roosevelt said, "no one can make you feel inferior without your consent."

1. "and so, my fellow Americans," said John F. Kennedy, "ask not what your country can do for you; ask what you can do for your country."

2. Gertrude Stein said, "a rose is a rose is a rose."

3. "what's in a name?" asked Romeo. "that which we call a rose by any other name would smell as sweet."

4. "always do right," said Mark Twain. "This will gratify some people and astonish the rest."

5. "in spite of everything, I still believe," Anne Frank said, "that people are really good at heart."

Practice

Work with a partner. Think of three questions to ask each other. Write your partner's answers as direct quotations. Try writing one of the answers as a divided quotation. When both of you are finished, check each other's writing for correct capitalization.

Review the answers to be sure your child has:

• written each answer as a direct quotation.

• written one answer as a divided direct quotation.

• used capital letters in quotations correctly.

_____

_____

_____

Tips for Your Own Writing: Proofreading.......................................

The next time you write a story, make sure to write a conversation for two or more of your characters. Capitalize the first word in each quotation and the first word in the second part of a divided quotation only when it begins a new sentence.

What do sentences and quotations have in common? Their first words are always capped.

9

Lesson 5

Lesson

5 Capitalization: Friendly and Business Letters

✏️ *The first words in certain parts of letters, such as greetings and closings, need capital letters.*

······················Did You Know?······················

There are two kinds of letters: friendly letters and business letters. Each kind of letter has its own form, but both letters have a greeting and a closing. The first word in a greeting is capitalized. So are any names or titles used in the greeting. Only the first word in a closing is capitalized.

Friendly Letter

1296 Meadow Drive
Glenview, IL 60025
August 17, 2000

Dear Teresa,
I have been home for a week, but it seems much longer! I really miss you and Rico. I had such a good time staying at your ranch.

Your friend,

Carolina

Business Letter

1296 Meadow Drive
Glenview, IL 60025
December 2, 2000

Appleby, Incorporated
1348 Forest Avenue
Houston, TX 77069

Dear Sir or Madam:
I am returning the sweater you sent. I ordered a Large and received a Small. Please send me the correct size.

Sincerely yours,
Carolina Ramirez
Carolina Ramirez

Show What You Know
Circle each word that should begin with a capital letter.

1. (dear) (aunt) (katherine)

2. (your) patient cousin,

3. (hope) to hear from you soon,

4. (dear) (mr.) (oglethorpe)

5. (sincerely)

6. (dear) (customer) (service) (department)

7. (yours) truly,

Score: _____   Total Possible: 14

10

Proofread
Here are two short friendly letters. There are five missing capital letters in each. Use the proper proofreading mark to show which letters should be capitalized.

Example: My aunt kathy will arrive in may.

129 Wickam Way
Hillville, NJ 08505
April 28, 2000

dear uncle fred,
mom told me that you fell down the back steps and sprained your ankle. I'm sending you several of my favorite books to help pass the time.

your nephew,

Wilson

4490 Main Street
Weston, IA 50201
may 4, 2000

dear wilson,
The books arrived, and i have already read one. Thank you for thinking of me. A sprained ankle is painful and boring!

love,

Uncle Fred

Practice
Think of a school or community problem. Write a letter to the editor of your local paper explaining the problem and your solutions to the problem. Write a draft of the body of your letter on the lines below. Then, using the business form, write the entire letter on a separate sheet of paper.

Review the letter to be sure your child has:

• written a letter to the editor.

• described a problem.

• offered solutions to the problem.

• used the business form for the letter.

• capitalized the appropriate words in the greeting and closing.

Tips for Your Own Writing: Proofreading
Look at a letter or note you have written recently. Check to see that you capitalized the appropriate words in the greeting and closing.

✏️ *A phone call is nice, but a letter is better!*

11

Lesson 6

Lesson

6 Review: Capitalization

A. Use the proper proofreading mark to fix thirty missing capital letters.

last saturday, which was august 23, my brother bill married suzanne. it's about time, too, because everyone has been working on that wedding since valentine's day! my sister jenny was the maid of honor, and i was an usher. it was hot, crowded, and uncomfortable. when rev. benson finally introduced mr. and mrs. william j. krupski, i wanted to cheer. of course, mom was crying, but then so were dad, aunt shirley, uncle dave, and lots of other people. maybe they were just glad it was over, as i was!

Score: _____   Total Possible: 30

B. Use the proper proofreading mark to show fifteen words (names of places, buildings, groups, religions) that should begin with capital letters.

In northwest cambodia, not far from its border with thailand, lies the ruined city of angkor. From about 880 to about 1225, angkor was the capital of the mighty Khmer Empire. The city has several temple complexes, all larger than the egyptian pyramids, that were built to honor hindu gods. The greatest of these temples is angkor wat. Its vast stone walls are covered with scenes from hindu mythology. Angkor was abandoned about 1434, and the capital was moved to phnom penh. Rediscovered by french missionaries in the 1860s and now regarded as one of southeast asia's great masterpieces, Angkor has begun to attract many tourists from the west.

Score: _____   Total Possible: 15

C. Write the titles from the title and paragraph below in the blanks on the following page, adding capital letters where they are needed. If the title is in italics, also underline it.

that versatile writer: edgar allan poe

Edgar Allan Poe wrote his first book *tamerlane and other poems* in 1827 when he was 18. He soon began writing fiction. Five of his stories were published in a newspaper, the *philadelphia saturday courier*, and a sixth story won a $50 prize. Poe then became editor of a magazine, the *southern literary messenger*. His story "the murders in the rue morgue" is considered to be the first classic detective story. Some of his poems, such as "the raven," are still well-known today.

12

---

1. _That Versatile Writer: Edgar Allan Poe_

2. _Tamerlane and Other Poems_

3. _Philadelphia Saturday Courier_

4. _Southern Literary Messenger_

5. _"The Murders in the Rue Morgue"_

6. _"The Raven"_

Score: _____   Total Possible: 6

D. Use the proper proofreading mark to add five capital letters where needed.

"senator Brock," the reporter asked, "do you know Hiram M. Douglas?"

"no, I do not," said Senator Brock. "the name is unknown to me."

"but look at this picture," insisted the reporter. "isn't that you and Douglas?"

Score: _____   Total Possible: 5

E. Use the proper proofreading mark under five lowercase letters that should be capitalized.

1422 Bristol Road
Columbus, OH 43221
may 22, 2000

dear kaitlin,
thank you for the birthday present. It was very clever of you to remember how much I liked Tina Weems's CD *Sweet Weems* and to give me a copy of my own. Isn't Tina supposed to have a new CD next month?

your friend,

Tyesha

Score: _____   Total Possible: 5

REVIEW SCORE: _____   REVIEW TOTAL: 61

13

Lesson 7

Lesson 7 — Punctuation: Sentences, Abbreviations, and Initials

Periods can be used to end a sentence, but they also let you know that a word is an abbreviation. That little dot is a valuable mark.

...Did You Know?...

A period is used at the end of a sentence that makes a statement.

Football is a popular sport.

A period is used after abbreviations for titles, the months of the year, and the days of the week.

Doctor—Dr.	Mister—Mr.	Senator—Sen.
October—Oct.	January—Jan.	December—Dec.
Friday—Fri.	Wednesday—Wed.	Monday—Mon.

A period is used after initials in names.

Susan Brownell Anthony—Susan **B.** Anthony
Booker Taliaferro Washington—Booker **T.** Washington

Show What You Know

Read the paragraph below. First, add periods at ends of sentences where needed. Then, change each bold word to an initial or abbreviation by adding a period and drawing a line through the unnecessary letters. Circle each period.

Early on **Saturday**, the first of **November**, Joseph **Andrew** Simon got into his car. Mr. Simon is a teacher at Lyndon **Baines** Johnson High School. Every **Monday** and **Wednesday** in **September** and **October**, he taught exercise classes for some heart patients of Dr. **Pablo** Gonzalez. These were held at Dwight **David** Eisenhower Elementary School. The classes were so popular that other programs hired him. Every **Tuesday** and **Thursday** morning, he worked at Gerald **Rudolph** Ford University. **Professor** Althea **Jane** Perkins sponsored the program. **Senator** Gutierrez and **Reverend** Tanaka participated in that class. Now each Saturday in November and **December**, Mr. Simon will be coaching a wheelchair basketball team in the James **Francis** Thorpe fieldhouse.

Score: _____ Total Possible: 23

14

Proofread

Read these notes for a report. Use proper proofreading marks to add nine missing periods.

Example: Dr. Bashir

Margaret H. Thatcher was born on Oct. 13, 1925. Mr. and Mrs. Alfred Roberts were her parents. The family lived in Grantham, Lincolnshire, England. After graduating, Margaret became a tax attorney and eventually was elected to Parliament in 1959. Becoming a member of Parliament is similar to being a senator in the United States government. Margaret Thatcher became the first woman leader of Britain's Conservative Party on Feb. 11, 1975. Four years later on May 3, 1979, she was elected Prime Minister. She resigned that post in Nov. of 1990.

Practice

Write notes to summarize the events of the school week. Write your notes in complete sentences, and use abbreviations when possible.

Review the notes to be sure your child has:
1. _____
   • put a period at the end of each sentence.
2. _____
   • put a period after each initial.
   • put a period after each abbreviation.
3. _____
   • written notes that make sense and relate to the topic.
4. _____
5. _____

Tips for Your Own Writing: Proofreading

Look for lists, notes, and other informal writing you have done. Check your writing to make sure you put a period at the end of sentences that are statements, and after initials, abbreviations, and each title.

Remember . . . periods put an end to statements and abbreviations.

15

Lesson 8

Lesson 8 — Punctuation: Other Abbreviations

Don't be fooled—there are some abbreviations that do not use periods!

...Did You Know?...

Two-letter postal abbreviations for state names do not have periods. See page 160 for a complete list.

Tennessee—TN	California—CA
Idaho—ID	New York—NY

Abbreviations for metric measurements do not have periods.

meter—m	kilogram—kg	milliliter—mL
liter—L	gram—g	kilometer—km

Initials for the names of organizations or companies do not use periods.

American Broadcasting Companies—ABC
Boy Scouts of America—BSA

Some terms that are made up of more than one word are known by their initials. These do not use periods.

videocassette recorder—VCR
gross national product—GNP

Show What You Know

Write the abbreviations or initials for the following items.

1. Indiana __IN__
2. milligram __mg__
3. Texas __TX__
4. centimeter __cm__
5. Illinois __IL__
6. Nevada __NV__
7. Maine __ME__
8. Washington __WA__
9. kiloliter __kl__
10. Florida __FL__
11. National Basketball Association __NBA__
12. recreational vehicle __RV__
13. American Heart Association __AHA__
14. World Health Organization __WHO__
15. Eastern Standard Time __EST__
16. Environmental Protection Agency __EPA__
17. decimeter __dm__
18. most valuable player __MVP__
19. North Dakota __ND__
20. Unidentified Flying Object __UFO__

Score: _____ Total Possible: 20

16

Proofread

Proofread this part of a report and change the bold words to abbreviations. Write the abbreviations on the lines below the report.

Hurricanes sweep the Gulf of Mexico during the summer months. The whirling storms can measure 200 to 300 **miles** (320 to 480 **kilometers**) in diameter. The eye of a hurricane travels at a speed of 10 to 15 **miles per hour**, or 16 to 24 kilometers per hour. The cloud forms may rise 10,000 **feet** (3048 **meters**) high and cover thousands of miles. One of the costliest hurricanes to strike the United States was Hurricane Andrew, which hit the Bahamas and headed **northwest** to **Florida** and **Louisiana** in 1992.

1. __mi.__
2. __km__
3. __mph__
4. __ft.__
5. __m__
6. __NW__
7. __FL__
8. __LA__

Practice

Find out about a storm in your state or imagine one that could hit. Write some notes using abbreviations. Your notes should be in complete sentences.

Review the notes to be sure your child has:
• put a period at the end of each sentence.
• used abbreviations in their notes.
• used the correct punctuation for each abbreviation.
• written notes that make sense and relate to the topic.

Tips for Your Own Writing: Proofreading

Look at some of your math papers or science reports to find examples of measurements. Check to see that you wrote the metric and customary measurement abbreviations correctly.

Abbreviations save time and space when you are taking notes or making lists.

17

Answer Key 125

Lesson 9

Lesson

9 Punctuation: End Marks

"*What does this say this is confusing*" *Can you read those sentences? Punctuation marks will make them clear!* "*What does this say? This is confusing.*"

···Did You Know?···

A period is used at the end of a sentence that makes a statement.

Machines help us with many daily tasks.

A period is used at the end of a sentence that gives an order or makes a request.

Turn on the dishwasher.

A question mark is used at the end of a sentence that asks a question.

How many machines do you use each day?

An exclamation point is used at the end of a statement, order, or request that expresses strong feeling.

That machine is awesome!
Pull that plug right now!

Show What You Know

Put the correct punctuation mark at the end of each sentence. Circle any periods you add so they will be easier to see.

Do you think robots will replace the workforce? I doubt it! However, many of tomorrow's jobs will be performed by robots. Think about the advantages this will bring for humans. They can do work that is dangerous for people to do. Noise, heat, smoke, and dust do not bother them. Neither does the freezing cold of outer space. A built-in computer controls a robot's actions so it can be programmed to do many difficult jobs.

The word *robot* comes from the Czech word *robota*, which means "drudgery." What does *drudgery* mean? It's work that is repetitive and tiresome. Robots don't care what the task is. They can work twenty-four hours a day at a steady pace. Best of all, they never make mistakes. How super! Robots never get bored and they never complain. They are truly special.

Score: _____   Total Possible: 17

18

Proofread

Use proofreading marks to add twelve end punctuation marks where they are needed.

Example: I love to swim.

Hiking is one of the most enjoyable forms of exercise. Walking is a form of hiking. Almost anyone can do it. All you really need is comfortable clothing and very comfortable walking shoes. Shoes are probably the most important hiking tool. You will be on your feet a lot, so take care of them. Get properly fitting shoes to avoid blisters and sore feet. It's also wise to check the weather report before you start. You can then select the correct type of clothing.

Find a special place to walk. It can be on a sidewalk in a park, a trail in the forest, or a path in the country. What can be better than walking along in a wooded area? Nothing on earth! As you walk, the sights and sounds of nature are all around you. You hear the leaves rustling. Are you listening to the birds? What beautiful sounds!

Practice

There are many kinds of exercise. What is your favorite? Write a paragraph about your favorite exercise that will convince your friends it is a great activity.

Review the paragraph to be sure your child has:

• written about a kind of exercise.

• given reasons to support the statement that the activity is great.

• put the correct punctuation mark at the end of each sentence.

Tips for Your Own Writing: Proofreading···

Select a story you have recently written. Check to see if you put periods after sentences that are statements, orders, or requests, question marks after questions, and exclamation points after sentences that express strong feelings.

Punctuation is the key to others understanding what you write. Use the right marks when you write!

19

···

Lesson 10

Lesson

10 Punctuation: Sentences

Sentences that run into each other need end punctuation. Use end punctuation marks to separate them.

···Did You Know?···

Two or more sentences written as though they were one sentence are hard to read. Correct use of end punctuation and capital letters will help you write better sentences.

Incorrect punctuation: Sundials, water clocks, and hourglasses were the earliest timekeepers they were made from natural materials in the A.D. 1000s, mechanical clocks were invented in China.

Correct punctuation: Sundials, water clocks, and hourglasses were the earliest timekeepers. They were made from natural materials. In the A.D. 1000s, mechanical clocks were invented in China.

A comma cannot be used as an end mark. Two sentences separated by only a comma are incorrectly punctuated.

Incorrect punctuation: Sundials tell time by measuring the angle of the shadow cast by the sun, hourglasses do not.

Correct punctuation: Sundials tell time by measuring the angle of the shadow cast by the sun. Hourglasses do not.

Show What You Know

Add periods where they are needed to correct the punctuation in this paragraph. Then circle the words that should be capitalized.

Early European mechanical clocks were huge. The gears of the mechanical clocks often occupied whole rooms. They had no dials or hands but marked the time by ringing a bell. These clocks, like other early clocks, were inaccurate. By 1400, the mechanical timekeeper had become a part of everyday life. Almost every town had an enormous "town clock."

Score: _____   Total Possible: 10

Proofread

The paragraph below has four places where the punctuation is incorrect. Correct the sentences by using proper proofreading marks to add four end punctuation marks and four capital letters.

Example: Seals are interesting animals. They are found in many parts of the world.

Harbor seals spend most of their time on floating ice chunks or land. Bearded seals enjoy spending their time in the same way. Harbor seals weigh between 100 and 150 pounds. They are usually about five feet in length. The weight of the larger bearded seals can be up to 1,500 pounds. They can grow to be twelve feet long. Harbor seals like to play in groups. Bearded seals are happy spending time alone. Seals have generally poor hearing, but their sight is good. Bearded seals have big, brushlike whiskers. Harbor seals have small, delicate ones.

Practice

Choose a pair of the animals in the picture and write a paragraph comparing them. How are they alike? How are they different? When you are finished, reread your paragraph to check for sentences that are missing end marks.

Review the paragraph to be sure your child has:

• explained how animals are alike and different.

• put a punctuation mark at the end of each sentence.

• avoided sentences that run on and on.

• used correct capitalization.

Tips for Your Own Writing: Proofreading···

The next time you write a report, check for sentences that need end marks. Read the sentences aloud to listen for mistakes in end punctuation.

Punctuation marks will help mark "the end" of sentences.

21

Lesson 11

Lesson 11 Punctuation: Sentence Fragments

"When I got on the bus." Is this a sentence? Add the missing parts to make a complete sentence.

Did You Know?

A sentence fragment is a group of words that is not a sentence. A *fragment* is a part of a sentence.

Fragment: Until it got dark.
Sentence: We played baseball until it got dark.

Fragment: After we ate dinner.
Sentence: After we ate dinner, we did our homework.

Show What You Know

Rewrite the paragraph to eliminate the sentence fragments. You can do this by adding the fragment to the beginning or end of the sentence it should be part of.

Itaipú, the most powerful electricity-producing dam in the world, is in Brazil. Paraguay and Brazil built the dam on the Paraná River. Which is in an area of dense tropical vegetation. The dam is 633 feet high and 5 1/2 miles long. After the dam was completed in 1991. The total cost of building it was determined to be $18 billion. The dam contains enough building materials to build a city for four million people. Because the water running over the dam sounds like music. It is called Itaipú, which means "singing dam" in Portuguese.

Itaipú, the most powerful electricity-producing dam in the world, is in Brazil. Paraguay and Brazil built the dam on the Paraná River, which is in an area of dense tropical vegetation. The dam is 633 feet high and 5 1/2 miles long. After the dam was completed in 1991, the total cost of building it was determined to be $18 billion. The dam contains enough building materials to build a city for four million people. Because the water running over the dam sounds like music, it is called Itaipú, which means "singing dam" in Portuguese.

Score: _____   Total Possible: 3

22

Proofread

Eliminate the three sentence fragments by adding the fragments to the beginning or end of a sentence.

George Washington Carver helped save farm industry in the South by showing farmers how to rotate crops. Which means to plant different crops from year to year. Through his bulletins and speeches. Carver taught farmers many things. He spent many years researching peanuts. Which was one of his great achievements.

1. George Washington Carver helped save farm industry in the South by showing farmers how to rotate crops, which means to plant different crops from year to year.

2. Through his bulletins and speeches, Carver taught farmers many things.

3. He spent many years researching peanuts, which was one of his great achievements.

Practice

Write a paragraph that tells what you believe to be the most exciting summer Olympic sport to watch. Give reasons for your choice. Be sure to use complete sentences.

Review the paragraph to be sure your child has:

• written a paragraph that makes sense and relates to the topic.

• avoided sentence fragments.

• put a punctuation mark at the end of each sentence.

• used correct capitalization.

Tips for Your Own Writing: Proofreading

Choose a favorite piece of your writing. Reading your work aloud can help you find sentence fragments. Some writers find it helps to "hear" problem sentence fragments if they read their papers "backwards," starting with the last sentence first.

Remember to make sentences "whole"—no parts or fragments allowed.

23

Lesson 12

Lesson 12 Review: Punctuation

A. Read these notes. Use the proper proofreading mark to add ten missing periods after sentences, abbreviations, and initials.

In an address to Congress in 1961, Pres. Kennedy called for a commitment to land a man on the moon before the end of the 1960s. Apollo 8 was launched on Dec. 21, 1968. Astronauts James A. Lovell, William Anders, and Frank Borman were on board. The spacecraft reached the moon on Tues. the 24th and proceeded to make ten orbits around the moon. Splashdown occurred early on Fri. the 27th of Dec.

Score: _____   Total Possible: 10

B. Write an abbreviation for each bold term.

In math class today we used formulas to change measurement systems. We changed **miles** (mi.) to **kilometers** (km) and **feet** (ft.) to **meters** (m). Then we used
    1   2   3   4
the map scale to measure the distance of the Oregon Trail from Independence,
Missouri (MO), to Fort Walla Walla, **Washington** (WA). Finally, we calculated the
          5   6
travel time on the trail for a wagon and a **recreational vehicle** (RV). We discovered that
                                                                7
the **miles per hour** (mph) were very different!
                      8

Score: _____   Total Possible: 8

C. Use the proper proofreading marks to add seven missing end punctuation marks to these directions.

Have you ever made homemade clay? These directions will help you create a small quantity of clay. Take one cup of warm water, one cup of salt, and two cups of cooking flour. Mix the ingredients together. Squeeze the wet flour until it is smooth and does not stick to your fingers. It's ready for modeling. You can create any type of sculpture you wish. You may also want to add food coloring to various batches to make colorful figures of clay. Have fun!

Score: _____   Total Possible: 7

24

D. The paragraph below has three incorrect sentences. Correct the sentences using proper proofreading marks to add three end punctuation marks and three capital letters.

For many years, people in the United States used streetcars to travel in cities. At first, streetcars called horsecars because they were pulled by horses. Later, streetcars were powered by steam in the 1800s. they began trying to use electric power, but making electricity was considered to be too expensive. In 1888 a machine was invented that made electricity inexpensively. In that same year, the first electric-powered streetcars were put into use. they quickly replaced the steam-powered streetcar. With the invention of the gas engine, electric streetcars were soon replaced by buses and cars. By 1930 the streetcar had begun to disappear from city streets. Interest in streetcars revived in the 1970s. streetcars use less energy per person and create less pollution than automobiles.

Score: _____   Total Possible: 6

E. Find and circle five sentence fragments. Then rewrite the paragraph by adding each fragment to the end of a sentence.

Garrett A. Morgan invented the gas mask. Morgan had to prove that his mask would work. Before people would use it. He showed a man going into a small tent. That was filled with smoke. The man stayed in the tent. For about twenty minutes. Next, the man went into a small room filled with poison gas. He stayed for fifteen minutes and was fine. When he came out. In 1916 Morgan used his gas mask to rescue more than twenty workers. Who were trapped in a smoke-filled tunnel in Cleveland.

Garrett A. Morgan invented the gas mask. Morgan had to prove that his mask would work before people would use it. He showed a man going into a small tent that was filled with smoke. The man stayed in the tent for about twenty minutes. Next, the man went into a small room filled with poison gas. He stayed for fifteen minutes and was fine when he came out. In 1916 Morgan used his gas mask to rescue more than twenty workers who were trapped in a smoke-filled tunnel in Cleveland.

Score: _____   Total Possible: 5

REVIEW SCORE: _____   REVIEW TOTAL: 36

25

Lesson 13

Lesson

13 Punctuation: Commas

Commas are the road signs writers use to separate things so they are easier to read.

.....................Did You Know?.....................

Commas are used to separate three or more items in a series. Put a comma after each item except for the last one.

Rolls, bagels, scones, and muffins are displayed in the bakery.
Customers can see, smell, and admire the different kinds of bread.
I bought carrot muffins, rye rolls, blueberry scones, and onion bagels.

Commas are used after introductory words such as *yes, no,* **and** *well.*

Yes, that bakery makes the best sourdough bread in the city.
Well, you have to get there early before the bread is gone.

An appositive follows a noun and gives more information about the noun. In the examples below, the appositives are in bold type. Commas are used to set off appositives from the rest of a sentence.

Mr. Schultz, **the bakery owner**, is very proud of his breads.
My favorite is pumpernickel, **a sour rye bread**.

Commas are used in direct address. Commas separate the name of the person spoken to from the rest of the sentence.

Do you have any wheat bread, Mr. Schultz?
Jerry, I put a loaf aside just for you.
You know, Mr. Schultz, you are a wonderful man!

....

Show What You Know
Read the paragraph. Add fourteen commas where they are needed.

Dogs come in all sizes, shapes, and colors. The American Kennel Club, the official dog breeding organization, recognizes 130 breeds in seven categories. For example, sporting dogs include pointers, setters, and retrievers. Collies, sheepdogs, and corgis are considered herding dogs. Ben, my boxer, is classified as a working dog. But to me, Ben is a companion. When I say, "Ben, come," he always comes. Well, maybe he doesn't *always* come. But he certainly comes when I say, "Dinner, Ben." Yes, *dinner* is definitely a word he knows!

Score: _____ Total Possible: 14

26

Proofread
Add eleven commas to this conversation where they are needed. Use the proper proofreading mark to show where each comma should be placed.

Example: Well, are you ready to begin?

"Lionel, I've got the telescope, two blankets, and some hot chocolate. Let's go outside and look at the moon, the stars, and the planets."

"Well, I don't know, Lucy. Will there be any snakes, spiders, or bats out there?"

"No, I don't think so, Lionel. Annie Callahan, my next-door neighbor, goes out star-gazing every night. So does Harry Thoreaux, your dentist. Last night he saw a meteor. Wouldn't you like to see a meteor, Lionel?"

"Yes, Lucy, I would. But only if I don't have to see any rats, roaches, or worms!"

"Then I suggest you look up, Lionel, rather than down!"

Practice
Write a paragraph in which you describe your favorite foods to a friend. In the first sentence, list at least three different foods. Then describe them. Use your friend's name in at least one sentence.

Review the sentences to be sure your child has:

• written sentences about his or her favorite foods.

• listed at least three foods and described them.

• addressed at least one of the sentences to a friend.

• used commas correctly with items in a series.

• used commas correctly in direct address.

Tips for Your Own Writing: Proofreading
Choose a piece of your own writing and ask a partner to proofread it, checking for commas between items in a series and with introductory words, appositives, and direct address.

Commas separate things to make your writing as clear as a bell.

27

Lesson 14

Lesson

14 Punctuation: Commas After Phrases and Clauses

Sentences are easier to read and understand when commas are used to set off phrases and clauses at the beginning of the sentences.

.....................Did You Know?.....................

A comma is used after a long prepositional phrase at the beginning of a sentence. A comma is not necessary if the prepositional phrase is very short. A prepositional phrase is a group of words that begins with a preposition such as *at, in, on,* **and** *of:*

On a beautiful August morning, Mark went climbing.
At noon he reached the mountain peak.
In 1998 Mark climbed his highest peak.

A comma is used after a subordinate clause at the beginning of a sentence. A subordinate clause is a group of words that begins with a subordinate conjunction such as *after, although, before, if, unless, when,* **and** *while.* **Even though the clause has a subject and a verb, it cannot stand alone as a sentence.**

After he got to the top, Mark sat down to rest.
While he was resting, he admired the view.

....

Show What You Know
Add seven commas where they are needed in this paragraph.

After La Salle explored the area, the French claimed the land in 1682 and called it Louisiana. After the French and Indian wars in the 1700s, France had to give Louisiana to Spain. In 1800 Spain had to give Louisiana back to France. Although Napoleon I wanted an American empire, he wanted money more. In 1803 he decided to sell Louisiana. For about $15 million, the United States could buy the land. When President Thomas Jefferson heard about the offer, he was delighted. Before Napoleon could change his mind, Jefferson bought the land. With one bold, decisive stroke, the United States doubled in size.

Score: _____ Total Possible: 7

28

Proofread
Read this paragraph and add four commas that are needed. Use the proper proofreading mark to show where each comma should be added.

Example: After grapes have been dried, they're called raisins.

If you want something good to eat, have some raisins. For a long, long time, I didn't like raisins. But one day there wasn't anything else to eat, so I popped a few raisins in my mouth. As I chewed, I realized, hey, these are good! Now I eat them all the time. At lunch I have a box for dessert. After a long day at school, I have a box as a snack. When I get the urge to munch, I go for the raisins. Without a doubt, I am now a raisin raver.

Practice
Describe what is happening in these pictures. Write your description on the lines below. Try to begin some of your sentences with subordinate conjunctions or prepositions.

Review the description to be sure your child has:

• described the given sequence of pictures.

• begun some sentences with subordinate conjunctions.

• used commas after long introductory prepositional phrases.

• used commas after introductory subordinate clauses.

Tips for Your Own Writing: Proofreading
The next time you write a report, check to see if you used any long phrases or clauses to introduce sentences and used commas to set off those phrases and clauses from the rest of their sentences.

Think of commas as places to pause briefly.

29

128 Answer Key

Lesson 15

Lesson 16

Lesson 17

Lesson 17 Punctuation: Dialogue—Commas and End Marks

Commas and periods always go within closing quotation marks. No questions asked. Exclamation points and question marks are open to question, aren't they?

........................Did You Know?........................

Commas and periods are *always* placed inside closing quotation marks.

"Until 1996," the sports fan said, "the Los Angeles Lakers held the record for the most team wins in a single season."

Question marks and exclamation points are placed inside the closing quotation marks if they are part of the quotation.

Her friend asked, "How many games did the Lakers win in one season?"

Question marks and exclamation points are placed outside the closing quotation marks if they are *not* part of the quotation.

How exciting to hear, "The Bulls broke the Lakers' record"!

Show What You Know

Add a total of twenty-nine quotation marks, commas, and end punctuation where they are needed in the sentences.

How excited Jan was when she heard the sportscaster say, "Last night the Chicago Bulls broke the team record for games won in a single season"!

"The Bulls broke the record," she shouted as she ran into my room.

I asked calmly, "What record did they break?"

Jan asked, "How could you not know? Don't you pay attention to sports?"

"No," I replied. "I don't pay much attention to sports."

How could I have known that Jan was about to give me a crash course in sports trivia when she said, "Come over here and sit down"?

"The Chicago Bulls just won seventy games for this season," Jan explained, "and that's the most games ever won in a single season by an NBA team."

Score: _____ **Total Possible: 29**

34

Proofread

Read this conversation between two sportscasters. Use proper proofreading marks to add eleven missing quotation marks, commas, and end punctuation marks.

Example: I told my family,^"^There is absolutely no sport as exciting as basketball!^"^

Bart said,^"^Listen to the crowd shouting!" The Chicago Bulls had just won their seventy-second game of the 1995–1996 season. "Who would have believed that we would be sitting here tonight announcing that the Chicago Bulls have established a new record for the most games won in a single season^?^

"Yes," said Bob. "it wasn't too long ago that people were asking whether the Bulls could break the record^.^

^"^Now that the Bulls have won their seventy-second game," said Bart,^"^people are asking me whether the Bulls' record can be broken^."^

Bob replied, "Only time will tell."

Practice

Think about an exciting sports event you have participated in or seen. Write a dialogue between you and a friend in which you talk about the event. Remember to start a new paragraph each time the speaker changes.

Review the account to be sure your child has:

* enclosed all dialogue within quotation marks.
* not enclosed the speaker's tag within the quotation marks.
* positioned the commas and periods within the quotation marks.
* placed question marks and exclamation points appropriately.
* written a dialogue that makes sense and relates to the topic.

Tips for Your Own Writing: Proofreading ....

The next time you write a story, include some dialogue. Make sure you place all periods and commas within closing quotation marks, and question marks and exclamation points outside quotation marks in quoted material.

In or out—"Watch your quotation marks and end punctuation!"

35

Lesson 18

Lesson 18 Punctuation: Direct and Indirect Quotations

Adam said, "Take it directly from me. This is a direct quotation." He then added that an indirect quotation restates something that was said.

........................Did You Know?........................

A <u>direct quotation</u> is the exact words someone said or wrote. A direct quotation is enclosed within quotation marks.

Abraham Lincoln said, **"A house divided against itself cannot stand."**

An <u>indirect quotation</u> is a restatement or rephrasing of something said or written. An indirect quotation is *not* enclosed in quotation marks.

Abraham Lincoln said that **a house in which there is no unity cannot withstand pressure from outside forces.**

An indirect quotation is often introduced by the word *that*, and a comma is not used to separate the speaker's tag from the indirect quotation.

Abraham Lincoln said **that** a house in which there is no unity cannot withstand pressure from outside forces.

Show What You Know

Decide whether each sentence includes a direct or an indirect quotation. If a sentence includes a direct quotation, add quotation marks where they are needed. If a sentence is an indirect quotation, write *indirect* on the line.

1. In one speech, Abraham Lincoln commented, "The ballot is stronger than the bullet." _____

2. Lincoln said in a campaign speech that no one would ever consider him a person who would become a President. _indirect_

3. "What is conservatism?" is a question Lincoln once asked. _____

4. Discouraged by news during the Civil War, Lincoln noted in 1861, "If McClellan is not using the army, I should like to borrow it for a while." _____

5. Lincoln stated that persons must stand firm in their important basic beliefs. _indirect_

6. In a letter to the editor, Lincoln noted that he supported giving the privileges of government to all those who helped bear the burdens of being involved in government. _indirect_

Score: _____ **Total Possible: 9**

36

Proofread

Read the article about Lincoln. It contains eight errors in punctuation involving direct and indirect quotations. Use proper proofreading marks to correct the errors.

Example: Mrs. Rainbucket said,^"^How about grabbing an umbrella?^"^ Mr. Hailstorm said that~~,~~ ~~"~~we could expect wet weather.~~"~~

Abraham Lincoln attended school less than a year but actually wrote his own math book. He said,^"^There were some schools, so called, but no qualification was ever required of a teacher, beyond readin', writin', and cipherin', to the Rule of Three.^"^

One book that made a lasting impression on Abe was *Life of Washington*. Of this book he said,^"^I recollect thinking then, boy even though I was, that there must have been something more than common that those men struggled for.^"^

Lincoln became a lawyer simply by reading law books to familiarize himself with the law. He said that~~,~~ ~~"~~If someone is resolutely determined to make a lawyer of himself, the thing is more than half done already.~~"~~

Practice

Imagine that you are a reporter who interviewed Abraham Lincoln during the Civil War. Write an article, using direct and indirect quotations.

Review the article to be sure your child has:

* enclosed only direct quotations within quotation marks, not the speaker's tag.
* positioned the end punctuation correctly within or outside the quotation marks.
* not used a comma or quotation marks with indirect quotations.
* written an article that makes sense and relates to the topic.

Tips for Your Own Writing: Proofreading ....

See if you can find a piece of your own writing that includes direct and indirect quotations. Make sure the speaker's tags are separated from direct quotations with commas, both opening and closing quotation marks are used, quotation marks with indirect quotations were avoided, and indirect quotations were introduced by the word *that*.

Knowing who said what and what was said puts a reader in the know!

37

Lesson 19

**Lesson
19 Punctuation: Friendly and Business Letters**

Are you sending a friendly or a business letter? The only major differences are that business letters have an inside address, and the greeting is followed by a colon.

......................Did You Know?......................

A friendly letter and a business letter both have distinct parts. The only difference in punctuation is following the greeting. A comma is used in a friendly letter and a colon in a business letter.

Friendly Letter

Heading →
8001 Colt Drive
Boise, ID 83709
September 7, 2000

Dear Katy, ← **Greeting**
Did you really rent a hot-air balloon? It must have been fun, but a bit frightening.
Please write and tell me about your adventure. ← **Body**

Sincerely, ← **Closing**
Glissia ← **Signature**

Business Letter

Heading →
854 Station Drive
Dunwoody, Georgia 30338
September 7, 2000

Balloons, Inc.
45 Martina Way
Dunwoody, Georgia 30338 **Inside Address**

Dear Ms. Bouchard: ← **Greeting**
What is the cost for 100 balloons in bunches of ten? ← **Body**

Sincerely, ← **Closing**
Glissia Shon ← **Signature**
Glissaia Shon ← **Printed name**
Event Manager ← **Title**

Show What You Know

Add punctuation where it is needed in this friendly letter to correct the four errors.

248 Sexton Drive
Mettawa, Illinois 60045
September 2, 2000

Dear Karin,
We made a hot-air balloon for our school play by attaching a plastic cloth to a cardboard box, and filling the cloth with helium-filled balloons. It looked great!
Your friend,
Madrena

Score: _____   Total Possible: 4

38

Proofread

Correct the punctuation in this business letter. Use proper proofreading marks to correct the five errors.

Example: Sea Isle City, FL 34746

513 Elm Wood Place
Kansas City, Missouri 64112
August 23, 2000

Country Music Association
One Music Circle South
Nashville, Tennessee 37203

Dear Music Director:

Our band, Country Nights, has played together for more than eight years. We have recently written and performed a new song that we think you will like. The song "Days into Nights" is recorded on the enclosed tape. Please let us know if you are interested in this song and others we have written.

Sincerely,
Mitch Fellfield
Mitch Fellfield
Manager, Country Nights Band

Practice

Think about a musical group that you would like to see perform. Write the body of a business letter to the group asking if they will be performing somewhere near you. Ask about prices, dates, and locations of the upcoming performances. On another sheet of paper, write your letter adding all the necessary parts.

Review the letter to be sure your child has:
• included a heading and inside address.
• used a colon after the greeting.
• used correct punctuation.

Tips for Your Own Writing: Proofreading

Choose a letter you have recently written. Check the letter to make sure it has the correct parts and is correctly punctuated.

Greetings to friends, use a comma in a letter. Greetings in business letters: use a colon.

39

Lesson 20

**Lesson
20 Review: Punctuation**

A. Use proper proofreading marks to add commas and quotation marks to each sentence. You will need to make sixteen corrections.

1. Homer wrote, "Your heart is always harder than a stone."

2. "Absence," Sextus Propertius wrote, "makes the heart grow fonder."

3. In *Othello*, Shakespeare wrote, "My heart is turned to stone."

4. "And what my heart taught me," wrote poet Robert Browning, "I taught the world."

5. "But it is wisdom to believe the heart," wrote George Santayana in one of his poems.

Score: _____   Total Possible: 16

B. Read the conversation below. Use proper proofreading marks to add end punctuation and quotation marks where they are needed. You will need to make nineteen corrections.

How did Vice-President Harry Truman feel when he heard Mrs. Franklin D. Roosevelt say, "Harry, the President is dead"?

He gave a clue, when he said to the press, "I felt like the moon, the stars, and all the planets had fallen on me."

"Harry Truman," our teacher said, "took over the presidency during World War II after President Roosevelt died from a stroke."

She then asked us, "How did Truman indicate that he knew the job of being President would be difficult?"

"His comments to the press," Mai answered, "showed that it would be difficult to replace Roosevelt."

Score: _____   Total Possible: 19

40

C. Use proper proofreading marks to add quotation marks to all direct quotations below. You will need to make sixteen corrections.

1. My younger brother asked, "How many planets are there?"

2. I told him that there were nine planets, and Earth was one of them.

3. Then he asked me if Earth was the largest planet.

4. "No," I told him, "Jupiter is the largest planet, and Earth is very small in comparison."

5. He continued to question me, asking, "Is Earth the smallest planet?"

6. I explained that Pluto was the smallest planet.

7. "But Earth is the best planet," he said.

8. "Yes, it is," I agreed, "because only on Earth can plants and animals live."

9. Then he told me that Earth was the best planet because I lived here.

10. I laughed and said, "No, Earth is the best because we both live here."

Score: _____   Total Possible: 16

D. Use proper proofreading marks to correct the nine errors in the paragraph below. Be sure to underline the names of books, plays, movies, newspapers, or magazines. Enclose the names of poems, articles, stories, or songs in quotation marks.

My partners and I are preparing a presentation about the Mississippi River. Jessica is reading a passage from Mark Twain's book <u>Life on the Mississippi</u>. Matt and Carlos are singing the song "Ol' Man River" from the play <u>Show Boat</u>. Sonia is reading part of the article "The Great Flood of 1993" that appeared in the October 1993 issue of <u>National Geographic World</u>. I am providing background information and closing the presentation with a poem that my partners and I wrote. It is called "The River of History."

Score: _____   Total Possible: 9

REVIEW SCORE: _____   REVIEW TOTAL: 60

41

Answer Key 131

Lesson 21

Lesson 21 — Usage: Verbs—Froze, Shook, Rang

Verbs, or action words, come in different forms. Which form do you use?

.....................Did You Know?.....................

A verb is an action or being word in a sentence. It tells what happens or what is. The form that you use depends upon the action that is being described. For example, the past form of a verb describes a past action. It usually consists of one word. The past participle form consists of the past form that is used with a helping verb such as *have, has, had, was,* or *were.*

Look at the present, past, and past participle forms of each of the troublesome verbs below. Then read the sentences that follow. They show correct usage for each form of these verbs.

Present	Past	Past Participle
Today they **freeze**.	Yesterday they **froze**.	They **have frozen**.
Today they **shake**.	Yesterday they **shook**.	They **have shaken**.
Today they **ring**.	Yesterday they **rang**.	They **have rung**.

We **froze** peach ice cream on the Fourth of July.
Dad **had frozen** the hamburger meat that he cooked on the grill.
We **shook** the whole way home after seeing the action movie.
The city residents **had been shaken** by the disasters that occurred.
Tina **rang** the dinner bell for the members of the camp.
She **has rung** that bell every evening for twenty years.

Show What You Know
Underline the correct form of each verb in parentheses.

Carlos was worried. He was sure he had (froze, <u>frozen</u>) the ice cream dessert long
1
enough. But would it be ready for the club members thirty minutes from now? Carlos took the
pan out of the freezer and (<u>shook</u>, shaken) it lightly. Well, no ripples disturbed the surface—a
2
good sign! Just then the phone (<u>rang</u>, rung): Dana was sick and couldn't come. After the
3
phone had (rang, <u>rung</u>) four more times, the meeting was off. Too many members were sick
4
or busy. "I (<u>froze</u>, frozen) that dessert for nothing," said Carlos. "But this has not
5
(shook, <u>shaken</u>) my confidence. I know I made a tasty treat!"
6

Score: _____ Total Possible: 6

42

Proofread
The following TV editorial uses the verb pairs *froze/frozen, shook/shaken,* and *rang/rung.* Each verb form is used incorrectly once. Using the proper proofreading marks, delete each incorrect word and write the correction above it.

Example: The people were ~~shook~~ shaken by the accident.

The people of this county have ~~froze~~ frozen through one of our worst winters, and earthquakes have ~~shook~~ shaken our homes. We cannot blame nature on politicians. But we can blame them for failing us. In a recent session, the state legislature ~~frozen~~ froze funds for earthquake relief. This act ~~shaken~~ shook our faith in the government.

Just one week ago, we ~~rung~~ rang in a new year. Let us resolve to shake up the government. Politicians, take notice: we have ~~rang~~ rung the alarm!

Practice
You may notice that the verbs in this lesson describe sensory actions. Write a strong sensory sentence for each verb in each pair. Use the same topic within each pair, but vary the sentences enough to make them interesting.

froze/frozen

Review the sentences to be sure your child has:
* written a sentence for each lesson verb.

shook/shaken
* written strong, evocative sensory sentences.
* written sentence pairs that are on the same topic.

rang/rung
* written sentences that make sense and are mechanically correct.

Tips for Your Own Writing: Proofreading..............................
Choose a piece of your own writing. See whether you find any of the three verb pairs from this lesson and if you used the correct form of each verb.

Froze, shook, and *rang* can stand by themselves, but *frozen, shaken,* and *rung* need a little help.

43

....

Lesson 22

Lesson 22 — Usage: Verbs—Swam, Tore, Took

Some verbs don't conform to the patterns we expect. Swam, swum? Tore, torn? Took, taken? How do you know which is right?

.........................Did You Know?.........................

The past form of a verb describes a past action. It usually consists of one word. The past participle form consists of the past form that is used with a helping verb such as *have, has, had, was,* or *were.*

Look at the present, past, and past participle forms of each of the troublesome verbs below. Then read the sentences that follow. They show correct usage for each form of these verbs.

Present	Past	Past Participle
Today they **swim**.	Yesterday they **swam**.	They **have swum**.
Today they **tear**.	Yesterday they **tore**.	They **have torn**.
Today they **take**.	Yesterday they **took**.	They **have taken**.

The bluefish **swam** together in a vast school off the coast.
They **have swum** along this coast for hundreds of years.
"You **tore** the jacket!" gasped the actress.
The curtain **was torn** from the stage in the scuffle that followed.
"I think you **took** more than your share," complained the hungry camper.
But she **had taken** exactly what was her due.

Show What You Know
Write the word that best completes each sentence.

The bluefin tuna __tore__ at its unfortunate prey. Then it __swam__ swiftly toward
1 (tore, torn) 2 (swam, swum)
another victim. That helpless fish had __torn__ one of its fins badly. A sea bass had
3 (tore, torn)
__taken__ a large shrimp for its dinner. The shrimp had __swum__ by lazily and carelessly.
4 (took, taken) 5 (swam, swum)
The hunter of the sea was no longer hungry, so it __took__ no more victims.
6 (took, taken)

Score: _____ Total Possible: 6

44

Proofread
The following radio script uses the verb pairs *swam/swum, tore/torn,* and *took/taken.* Using the proper proofreading marks, delete four incorrect words and write the correction above each one.

Example: We ~~swum~~ swam for an hour.

NARRATOR: Here comes our hero, Pam Pekinese. Pam has swum across the lagoon in record time. (*Sound effect for swimming.*)

PAM: I have ~~swum~~ swam my last mission! It's true that I'm the world's greatest swimming Pekinese, but I have ~~took~~ taken all I can take! See? Those playful dolphins ~~torn~~ tore two of my favorite hair ribbons. Yap, yip.

MEL MYNAH: You didn't expect any dolphins you swam by to pass up a chance to tease you? They did the same thing when you ~~swum~~ swam by them last week.

NARRATOR: Tune in next week for "Strange Animals Do Strange Things."

Practice
Write a brief description of a giant squid attacking a boat at sea. Use all the verb pairs presented in this lesson. Choose other words carefully to give the story a strong sense of action.

Review the description to be sure your child has:
* used all of the verbs from this lesson.
* used action-packed verbs and colorful, descriptive adjectives and adverbs.
* written sentences that relate to the topic and are mechanically correct.

Tips for Your Own Writing: Proofreading..............................
Choose a sample of your own writing. Look for *took/taken, swam/swum,* and *tore/torn.* Check to see that you used a helping verb with *taken, swum,* and *torn.*

If you swam through this lesson without hitting a snag, you have swum well!

45

132 Answer Key

Lesson 23

Lesson

23 Usage: Verbs—Wrote, Stole, Began

Troublesome verbs refuse to conform. You have to learn them one by one—or two by two!

.....................Did You Know?.....................

The past form of a verb describes a past action. It usually consists of one word. The past participle form consists of the past form that is used with a helping verb such as *have, has, had, was,* or *were.*

Look at the present, past, and past participle forms of each of the troublesome verbs below. Then read the sentences that follow. They show correct usage for each form of these verbs.

Present	Past	Past Participle
Today they **write.**	Yesterday they **wrote.**	They **have written.**
Today they **steal.**	Yesterday they **stole.**	They **have stolen.**
Today they **begin.**	Yesterday they **began.**	They **have begun.**

"Where is the poem that I **wrote?**" bellowed Milton.
The weary poet **had written** many stanzas last night.

Someone **stole** Hannah's gym shoes.
My favorite sneakers **were stolen** from the gym, also.

The mourning dove **began** its sorrowful song.
The birds **had begun** their chorus at 4:30 in the morning!

Show What You Know
Read the paragraph. Underline the correct form of each verb in parentheses.

In an ancient land called Sumer, scholars (<u>wrote</u>, written) on clay tablets with a stylus. The
                                                ¹
stylus was a tool that made wedge-shaped marks in wet clay. Young students (<u>began</u>, begun)
                                                                                  ²
their education by learning to write with this tool. Why did the Sumerians develop this type of

writing? One reason was that they had (began, <u>begun</u>) to record laws. Writing down a code of
                                              ³
laws allows a society to apply laws equally. For example, Sumerian judges could punish any

powerful person who (<u>stole</u>, stolen) goods the same as anyone else who had (stole, <u>stolen</u>).
                        ⁴   ⁵
Soon, people found easier ways to write. Keepers of records have not (wrote, <u>written</u>) on clay
                                                                                  ⁶
tablets for centuries!

Score: _____   Total Possible: 6

46

Proofread
The following interview uses the verb pairs *wrote/written, stole/stolen,* and *began/begun.*
Each verb form is used incorrectly once. Using the proper proofreading mark, delete each
incorrect word and write the correction above it.

Example: We ~~begun~~ our day early. *(began)*

INTERVIEWER: Tell us what you have ~~wrote~~ lately, Pete. *(written)*

PETE PORTER: Well, Zara, I have been writing an epic poem about the dawn of the computer

age. Some critics might claim that I ~~stolen~~ the idea from Beryl Brinkley, but *(stole)*

that's not true.

INTERVIEWER: Critic Natalie Naster claimed that you had ~~stole~~ the rhymes. But enough of *(stolen)*

that. You ~~written~~ ten short poems last year, didn't you? *(wrote)*

PETE PORTER: Right. But now I have ~~began~~ to create epic poetry! *(begun)*

INTERVIEWER: Fascinating. When you ~~begun~~ your career, we had no idea you'd write epic *(began)*

poetry. We look forward to your new poem.

Practice
**Imagine the dispute between poets Pete Porter and Beryl
Brinkley. Write a short letter that one of these poets might write
to the other one. Include the verbs presented in this lesson.**

Review the letter to be sure your child has:
• used at least three of the verbs from this lesson.
• used language that conveys some of the emotional content of
  a dispute.
• written sentences that relate to the topic and are mechanically correct.

Tips for Your Own Writing: Proofreading..................................
Choose a story you have written. See whether you find any of the three verb pairs from this lesson.
Make sure you used a helping verb when necessary.

*"Wrote/written, stole/stolen, began/begun—
Learning verbs in pairs can be lots of fun!"*

47

Lesson 24

Lesson

24 Usage: Verbs—Blew, Sank, Fell

Studying past forms of verbs in pairs gives us clues to solving verb mysteries. Elementary, my dear Watson!

.....................Did You Know?.....................

The past form of a verb describes a past action. It usually consists of one word. The past participle form consists of the past form that is used with a helping verb such as *have, has, had, was,* or *were.*

Look at the present, past, and past participle forms of each of the troublesome verbs below. Then read the sentences that follow. They show correct usage for each form of these verbs.

Present	Past	Past Participle
Today they **blow.**	Yesterday they **blew.**	They **have blown.**
Today they **sink.**	Yesterday they **sank.**	They **have sunk.**
Today they **fall.**	Yesterday they **fell.**	They **have fallen.**

The wind **blew,** slapping rain across the deck.
Fiercer gales **had blown** before.

One storm last fall **sank** a freighter ten miles off the coast.
But no ship of mine **has** ever **sunk.**

In a shocking crash, the main mast **fell** to the deck!
It **had fallen** so suddenly, no one could sound a warning.

Show What You Know
In each pair of sentences, draw a line to match each sentence with the verb form that it should use.

The BBW Story (Big Bad Wolf)

1. The BBW had a reputation to keep up: he ____ houses down. —— blown
   This wouldn't be the first straw hut he had ____ away. —— blew

2. But when the pigs heard him, their hearts had ____ to their toes. —— sank
   Before hiding, they ___ their valuables into the well. —— sunk

3. What was the outcome? The house had ___—no big deal. —— fallen
   "We really ___ for that huff-and-puff story," said Pig Junior. —— fell

Score: _____   Total Possible: 6

48

Proofread
The following is an imaginary diary entry by a sailor in the 1700s. The writer used the verb pairs
blew/blown, sank/sunk, and *fell/fallen* incorrectly six times. Using the proper proofreading
mark, delete each incorrect word and write the correction above it.

Example: The sun ~~sunk~~ below the horizon. *(sank)*

At about 9:00 A.M., a gust of wind ~~blown~~ suddenly, shaking the ship to its keel. Just then *(blew)*

the second mate fell to the deck. Others had ~~fell,~~ too, so great was the jolt. The tempest blew, *(fallen)*

and then it had ~~blew~~ some more. Another dreadful gust hit. "Have we ~~sank~~ for good?" cried *(blown)* *(sunk)*

the first mate. "The enemy never ~~sunk~~ this scow," shouted Captain Cruz, "nor will Mother *(sank)*

Nature now!" When the wind had ~~fell,~~ we knew that the ship had not sunk. *(fallen)*

Practice
**Imagine that you are at sea on a boat like the one in the
picture. Suddenly, an intense storm blows up. Describe the
experience, using strong action verbs and vivid descriptive
words. Also, use the three pairs of verbs presented in this
lesson.**

Review the paragraph to be sure your child has:
• used at least three of the verbs from this lesson.
• used other strong action verbs and vivid adjectives.
• written sentences that relate to the topic and are mechanically correct.

Tips for Your Own Writing: Proofreading..................................
Review a report you have written. Look for the words *blew/blown, sank/sunk,* and *fell/fallen.* Check the
sentences to see that you have used a helping verb with *blown, sunk,* and *fallen.*

*You neither sank nor fell in this lesson, nor have you sunk or fallen! If you blew your own
horn, then you have blown it for good reason.*

49

Lesson 25

Lesson

25 Usage: Verbs—Lie/Lay, Rise/Raise

✏️ *Many writers have trouble with these tricky verb pairs. See whether you can beat the averages!*

······································Did You Know?·····························

The following word pairs have related meanings that invite confusion. Read on to learn how to use them correctly.

Lie means "to be at rest or recline." *Lay* means "to put or to place (something)."

> Beth just wanted to **lie** on the beach for a whole week.
> You should **lay** your beach towel on the sand away from the surf.

Rise means "to move in an upward direction." *Raise* means "to lift (something)" or "to move something higher."

> The moon should **rise** in the early evening, according to the script.
> Jenny tugged on the rope to **raise** the cutout moon in the theater set.

···

Show What You Know

Correctly fill in each blank with one of these words: *lie, lay, rise, raise.*

A Night in Camp

I am happy as I ____*lie*____ on the air mattress, gazing at the brilliant, starry sky. I feel I
                    1
could grab the low, oval moon and ____*lay*____ it here beside me. Instead, I ____*lie*____ very still.
                                    2   3
No noise disturbs the quiet. No breeze rustles the leaves above. Nearby, I see smoke ____*rise*____
                                                                                       4
lazily from the dying campfire. It curls and twists up to the leafy ceiling of tree limbs.
Hypnotized, I watch it ____*rise*____ higher and then disappear. When I ____*raise*____ my head a
                        5   6
little, I see that the embers have at last died out. I want to wake up before dawn so that I can
see the sun ____*rise*____. All is well in camp. This is the life!
            7

Score: _____   Total Possible: 7

50

Lesson 25 (right page)

Proofread

The following bread recipe uses the verbs *lie/lay* and *rise/raise* incorrectly four times. Using the proper proofreading mark, delete each incorrect word and write the correct word above it.

Example: Does the cookbook lay̶ on the table? *(lie)*

Della's Old-Fashioned Bread

1. Mix the yeast, sugar, and warm water in a small bowl. Put the bowl in a warm place for the
   yeast to rai̶s̶e̶. *(rise)*

2. In a separate bowl, mix the flour and salt. Li̶e̶ this bowl aside for now. *(Lay)*

3. After ten minutes, mix everything together in a large bowl. Make a ball of dough.

4. If the dough will la̶y̶ in your hand without sticking, it is just right. If not, add flour. *(lie)*

5. Put the dough on your board. Ri̶s̶e̶ your hand and push your palm into the dough. Raise your
   hand and repeat the action. (This action is called "kneading" the dough.) *(Raise)*

Practice

Look at the drawing. What time of year does it suggest? Write a brief story or description in response to this picture. Use the verb pairs *lie/lay* and *rise/raise.*

Review the story or description to be sure your child has:

• used the verbs *lie, lay, rise,* and *raise.*

• chosen words to convey the feelings he or she remembers

  from having experienced such a fall evening.

• written sentences that make sense and are mechanically correct.

_____

_____

_____

_____

Tips for Your Own Writing: Proofreading

Choose a piece of your own writing. Look for the verbs *lie* and *lay.* Check to see that *lie* is used when you mean "to be at rest" and *lay* when you mean "to put or place." Look for other troublesome word pairs such as *rise* and *raise.*

✏️ *Don't lie down on the job, don't lay your troubles down, and don't raise your voice. Just rise to the occasion! Get it?*

51

···

Lesson 26

Lesson

26 Usage: Verbs—Can/May, Let/Leave, Teach/Learn, Bring/Take

✏️ *With some confusing verb pairs, we just have to learn and remember the difference. It's hard work, but the payoff is appropriate usage!*

······································Did You Know?·····························

The following word pairs have related meanings that invite confusion.

Can means "to be able to (do something)." *May* means "to be allowed or permitted to (do something)."

> **Incorrect:** "**Can** I be excused?" asked Carmen.
> **Correct:** "**May** I be excused?" asked Carmen.

Let means "to allow." *Leave* means "to depart" or "to permit something to remain where it is."

> **Incorrect:** "**Leave** me go!" begged the caged animal's eyes.
> **Correct:** "**Let** me go!" begged the caged animal's eyes.

Teach means "to explain" or "to help (someone) understand." *Learn* means "to gain knowledge."

> **Incorrect:** Please **learn** me how to tie a square knot.
> **Correct:** Please **teach** me how to tie a square knot.

Bring means "to fetch" or "to carry toward (oneself, something, or someone)." *Take* means "to carry in a direction away from (oneself, something, or someone)."

> **Incorrect:** **Bring** your mom to that countryside restaurant.
> **Correct:** **Take** your mom to that countryside restaurant.

···

Show What You Know

Underline the correct form of each verb in parentheses.

1. (<u>Can</u>, May) I speak six languages? Yes, (can, <u>may</u>) I show you now?

2. (Leave, <u>Let</u>) me just say this before I have to (<u>leave</u>, let).

3. Teachers want to (<u>teach</u>, learn) their pupils. Pupils want to (teach, <u>learn</u>) from them.

4. (Bring, <u>Take</u>) your lunch, but (take, <u>bring</u>) me the extra money.

Score: _____   Total Possible: 8

52

Lesson 26 (right page)

Proofread

The following report contains the verbs presented in this lesson. In six places, those verbs are used incorrectly. Using the proper proofreading mark, delete each incorrect word and write the correction above it.

Example: Le̶a̶v̶e̶ us do the work. *(Let)*

The Chinese write their language in a different way than people write their languages in
the West. They do not use an alphabet, if you ma̶y̶ imagine that. Instead, the Chinese learn a *(can)*
unique character for every word. There are about fifty thousand characters in all. Imagine
having to learn all those characters or having to lea̶r̶n̶ them to someone else. In fact, educated *(teach)*
Chinese can read thousands of characters. This knowledge will lea̶v̶e̶ them read a newspaper *(let)*
easily.
    Ca̶n̶ I tell you one more thing? I am studying Chinese, and I will bri̶n̶g̶ you to my class if *(May)* *(take)*
you'd like. Just be sure to ta̶k̶e̶ an open mind with you. *(bring)*

Practice

Write one sentence for four of the verbs introduced in this lesson. Then use a dictionary to find definitions for these verbs that are different from the ones presented here. Write a sentence for each different definition you find.

Review the sentences to be sure your child has:

• written a sentence for four of the eight verbs *can, may, let,*

  leave, teach, learn, bring, and *take.*

• located different definitions of the words (*can:* to put up by the

  canning process; *may:* to admit possibility; *let:* to rent; *leave:* to bequeath; *teach:* to instruct

  in school; *learn:* to become aware of, and so on).

_____

_____

Tips for Your Own Writing: Proofreading

The next time you write a story or report, be aware of how you can use *can* and *may.* Remember, *can* means "to be able to" and *may* means "to be allowed to."

✏️ *May I congratulate you on this lesson? You can now ace these difficult verbs!*

53

134 Answer Key

Lesson 27

Lesson

27 Review: Verbs

A. The following is a fictional account of an expedition to the South Pole. Underline the correct form of each verb in parentheses.

The expedition consisted of Woods, Danner, and Abaji, the captain. On December 1, the crew (<u>began</u>, begun) its trek inland across the ice shelf. The first mishap occurred that very day.
1
One of the dogs lost its footing and (<u>fell</u>, fallen) into the icy water. Though it (<u>swam</u>, swum) to
2   **3**
safety, the dog (<u>shook</u>, shaken) all over and was badly chilled. That night, the wind
4
(<u>blew</u>, blown) with a terrible force. Earlier, it had (blew, <u>blown</u>) down one of the tents in camp.
5   **6**
The crew soon learned that a gust had (tore, <u>torn</u>) this tent beyond repair. The very next day,
7
they watched helplessly as one of the supply sleds (sank, <u>sunk</u>) into a crevasse. Weighted down
8
with food, it had (sank, <u>sunk</u>) with terrifying speed. Hungry and engulfed by bitter cold, the
9
party (<u>fell</u>, fallen) into despair.
10
Three days later, all but one had (froze, <u>frozen</u>) to death. This was Captain Abaji, who
11
(<u>wrote</u>, written) in his diary every day. His last entry was "We have (fell, <u>fallen</u>) Here I have
12   **13**
(wrote, <u>written</u>) the truth: we perished with courage."
14

Score: _____   Total Possible: 14

B. Decide whether the underlined word in each sentence is used correctly. If it is, put a C above the word. If it is not, write the correct word above the underlined word.

                            C   took
Brett had <u>stolen</u> a candy bar from his sister Ann's lunch box. He <u>taken</u> it without thinking
1   **2**
                            tore
about his action. As he <u>torn</u> off the wrapper, he realized what he'd done. Though the candy
                     3
                 C   C
looked tasty, Brett <u>began</u> to feel very ashamed. He <u>wrote</u> a note of apology to put in Ann's
4   **5**
                                      frozen
lunch box with the candy bar. Just then, Ann came into the kitchen. Brett was <u>froze</u> in his tracks.
                                                       6

Score: _____   Total Possible: 6

54

C. In each blank, write a verb from the list. Some verbs may be used more than once. Some may not be used at all.

raise	rise	take	bring	let	leave	can	may	lie	lay

Clyde's Bad Break in Show Biz

MS. DÍAZ: Please ___bring___ something to school for your demonstration speech.
             1

LOU: ___May___ I bring my pet snake Clyde? It will ___lie___ quietly in one place and
     2   **3**
       not bother a soul. We'll only have to worry if we see it ___raise___ its tail.
                                         4

MS. DÍAZ: But ___can___ your snake bite?
             5

LOU: Maybe. But I'll tell Clyde: "You ___may___ not bite!"
                               6

MS. DÍAZ: Thanks, but I cannot ___let___ Clyde come to school. You will have to ___leave___
                                   7   **8**
       your talented snake at home.

Score: _____   Total Possible: 8

D. Write the verb in the parentheses that correctly completes each sentence.

1. (rang, rung) The year is 1905. The school bell has just ___rung___. The teacher ___rang___ that bell by hand at the same time yesterday.

2. (teach, learn) The one-room schoolhouse is full of youngsters eager to ___learn___. The school has one teacher. She will ___teach___ students of all ages.

3. (lie, lay) The students sit down and ___lay___ their hands together on their desks. No one will slouch or ___lie___ down in this schoolroom!

4. (rise, raise) To ask a question, students must ___raise___ their hands. The teacher says, "Yes, Maude (or Clarence), you may ___rise___."

5. (bring, take) There is no lunchroom. Students ___bring___ cold food from home to school. They ___take___ the leftovers home after the closing bell rings.

Score: _____   Total Possible: 10

REVIEW SCORE: _____   REVIEW TOTAL: 38

55

Lesson 28

Lesson

28 Usage: Adjectives

✎ *Writing—and life—would be dull without comparisons. We have rules in English for how to compare using adjectives.*

.................................Did You Know?.................................

Adjectives—words that modify nouns or pronouns—use different forms when used to make comparisons. The <u>comparative</u> form of an adjective is used to compare two things.
    This fish is **larger** than that one.   Sara is **more talkative** than Li.

The <u>superlative</u> form of an adjective is used to compare more than two things.
    The Siberian tiger is the **largest** member of the cat family.
    The **most talkative** person I've ever known is Kareem.

Did you notice two of the adjectives end with *-er* or *-est* and the other two adjectives use *more* or *most*? Short adjectives usually add *-er* or *-est*. Longer adjectives usually add *more* or *most*.

Most adjectives are *regular*: they follow the above patterns in forming their comparatives and superlatives. But a few adjectives are *irregular*: they form their comparatives and superlatives in different ways.

Regular Adjectives	Comparative Adjectives	Superlative Adjectives
good	better	best
bad	worse	worst

The only way to learn these irregular forms is to memorize them.

Show What You Know

Rewrite each adjective in bold type. Write it in the blank in either the comparative or superlative form.

1. On the tennis court, Mei is a **powerful** opponent. Is she ___more powerful___ than Jo?

2. But Jo has a **strong** backhand. It may be ___stronger___ than Mei's.

3. They are both **good** players. But which one is ___better___?

4. Their match was a **long** one. It was the ___longest___ match in the tournament.

5. It was also **exciting**. It was the ___most exciting___ match I saw all week.

Score: _____   Total Possible: 5

56

Proofread

In the following report, underline the five adjectives that are used in their comparative or superlative form. For each of the four forms used incorrectly, use the proper proofreading mark to delete it and write the correction above it.

                  slower
Example: A car moves ~~more slow~~ than a train.

The pyramid is a basic form in geometry. Human beings have built pyramids as tombs or
                                                             tallest
places of worship throughout history. Of all the pyramids in the world, the <u>~~taller~~</u> one is King

Khufu's Great Pyramid in Egypt. It rises more than 450 feet (137 meters). Some people
                   most beautiful
consider this the <u>~~beautifulest~~</u> as well as the <u>largest</u> pyramid.

Native Americans also built many pyramids. American pyramids had a stair-stepped side
                        most complete
and a flat top. The <u>~~completest~~</u> one today is the Temple of Inscriptions at Palenque, Mexico.
                                             shorter
Though quite beautiful, this structure is much <u>~~more short~~</u> than Egypt's Great Pyramid.

Practice

Write a story using at least five comparative or superlative adjectives.

Review the story to be sure your child has:

• used at least five adjectives in comparative and
  superlative forms.

• used expressive action verbs and colorful modifiers in addition
  to the required adjectives.

• written a story that makes sense and is mechanically correct.

_____

_____

_____

_____

Tips for Your Own Writing: Proofreading.................................

The next time you write a description in a story, be sure you use *-er* or *more* with adjectives when comparing two things, and *-est* or *most* with adjectives when comparing more than two things.

✎ *When comparing two, use two letters (-er); when comparing three or more, use three letters (-est).*

57

Lesson 29

Lesson
29 Usage: Adverbs

Add spice to your writing with adverbs—especially adverbs of comparison.

................................**Did You Know?**................................

Adverbs—words that modify verbs, adjectives, or other adverbs—use different forms when used to make comparisons. The **comparative** form of an adverb is used to compare two actions.

> Deb arrived **later** than Heather.
> Bill shuffled his test papers **more noisily** than Tyrone.

The **superlative** form of an adverb is used to compare more than two actions.

> Jewel climbed the **highest** of all.
> Of all the students, Ernesto worked the **most rapidly.**

Short adverbs add *-er* or *-est.*

Most adverbs that end in *-ly* form their comparatives and superlatives using *more* and *most.* A few that do not end in *-ly* also use *more* and *most.*

> I eat olives **more often** than Mom, but Dad eats them the **most often.**

Most adverbs are *regular:* they follow the above patterns in forming their comparatives and superlatives. A few adverbs are *irregular.*

> **Regular:** The Badgers played **badly** in the play-offs.
> **Comparative:** The Tigers played **worse** than the Bears.
> **Superlative:** Of all the teams, the Lions played the **worst.**

....

Show What You Know
Rewrite the adverb in the bold type. Write it in the blank in either the comparative or superlative form.

1. Our hockey team skated **badly.** We skated _____worse_____ than we usually do.

2. The coach arrived at the rink **late.** The goalie arrived _____latest_____ of all.

3. Carl missed the goal **frequently.** He also shot _____more frequently_____ than others.

4. Our fans cheered **noisily.** Of all the schools' fans, we cheered the _____most noisily_____.

Score: _____ **Total Possible: 4**

58

Proofread
In the following school newspaper article, underline the eight adverbs that are used in the comparative or superlative form. For the four forms used incorrectly, use the proper proofreading mark to delete the word and write the correction above it.

Example: That race is ~~more easy~~ than this one. *(easier)*

   The Science Club sponsored a Turtle Derby last Thursday. Three candidates—Ralph, Ed, and Trixie—lined up at the starting gate. At the pop of a balloon, they were off! Trixie moved slowly to start. But Ralph moved more slowly than Trixie. Ed moved the ~~more slowly~~ *(most slowly)* of the three. (It was clear that Trixie took the race ~~seriouser~~ *(more seriously)* than Ralph.)

   When interviewed, a spectator, Perry Plum, said: "Trixie started badly, but Ed started worse than she did. Ralph started the ~~baddest~~ *(worst)* of the three." Not everyone agreed. Tilly Towson said, "I rate Trixie pretty high, Ed higher than Trixie, and Ralph the highest of all!"

   So who won? The turtle who tried ~~most hard~~ *(hardest)*—Trixie, of course.

Practice
Look at the picture. Write a description of the skier's run down the ski slope. Use at least two adverbs in their comparative or superlative form.

Review the description to be sure your child has:

• used at least two adverbs in comparative and superlative forms.

• captured the feeling of elation that one experiences when engaged in a challenging (sometimes even dangerous) physical activity.

• used the adverbs appropriately (they should convey feelings similar to those described previously).

Tips for Your Own Writing: Revising...
Choose a piece of your own writing. Exchange it with a partner to find the adverbs. Then, look for places to use adverbs that compare. Revise your writing.

What have you done superbly? Then think of something you did more superbly, and finally, something you did the most superbly of all!

59

- -

Lesson 30

Lesson
30 Usage: Good/Well, Bad/Badly

Good and well are as tangled as a plate of spaghetti! Read on to untangle them. (Thank goodness bad and badly are pretty straightforward.)

................................**Did You Know?**................................

Good and *bad* are adjectives. Use them to modify nouns or pronouns. Sometimes they follow the verb. *Well* and *badly* are adverbs. Use them to modify verbs, adjectives, or other adverbs.

> I helped Raoul choose a **good** book.
> I feel **good** about the food we collected for homeless people.
> Mrs. Choy told me that Raoul read **well** in class.
> We had a **bad** thunderstorm last night.
> The weather forecaster predicted **badly.**

The word *well* is a special problem. It usually functions as an adverb, but it can be an adjective when it is used to mean "healthy." Usually, the adjective *well* follows a linking verb such as *am.*

> **Adverb:** Marita sang **well** at her concert last night.
> **Adjective:** "I am **well,**" replied Ms. Slocum.

Remember that *good* is *always* used as an adjective. Also, remember that "feeling good" describes a state of mind, while "feeling well" describes someone's health.

Show What You Know
Underline the correct word in each word pair in parentheses.

Weightlessness is a potential health problem in space travel. Muscles can weaken (bad, <u>badly</u>)₁ if astronauts fail to exercise enough. Another (<u>bad,</u> badly)₂ effect is that the heart may get larger. On the other hand, some astronauts say that weightlessness makes them feel (<u>good,</u> badly)₃. It brings on a mood of contentment. Scientists have found ways to help people cope with weightlessness. So, if you should meet an astronaut, ask, "How are you? Are you (good, <u>well</u>)₄ today?" Maybe she or he will answer, "I'm fine. I have coped (good, <u>well</u>)₅ with weightlessness."

Score: _____ **Total Possible: 5**

60

Proofread
Bonita Bower's campaign speech has been published. It has five errors in it. Using the proper proofreading mark, delete each incorrect word and write the correction above it.

Example: The runner ran ~~good~~ *(well)* in the race.

   Good evening. I'm running for mayor. During the last election, I was defeated ~~bad~~ *(badly)*. But since then, I have talked to many people from all walks of life. And I feel ~~well~~ *(good)* about that. I've learned that we must all take an interest in city government.

   I support conservation. As mayor, I will educate my staff to use supplies wisely. If we do ~~good~~ *(well)* at this, I will not request an increase in office budgets for two years.

   I also want to improve public transportation. Service isn't always very ~~well~~ *(good)*. People who work far from home and don't drive are getting a ~~badly~~ *(bad)* deal.

   Please vote for me, Bonita Bower, next Tuesday. I promise to do a good job!

Practice
Look at the picture. Have you ever thought about how difficult it must be to perform simple, daily tasks in space? Use your imagination to think of a way that this young astronaut could solve his problem. Use the word pairs introduced in this lesson.

Review the paragraph to be sure your child has:

• used *good/well* and *bad/badly* correctly.

• chosen action verbs and modifiers carefully.

• created imaginative solutions to the problem posed in the art.

• written sentences that make sense and are mechanically correct.

Tips for Your Own Writing: Proofreading...
Choose a piece of your own writing. Look for the words *good, well, bad,* and *badly.* Make sure that you used *good* and *bad* to describe nouns and pronouns, and *badly* to describe verbs, adjectives, and other adverbs. Pay particular attention to the word *well.*

Did you do well in this lesson? Then you should feel good about it!

61

136 Answer Key

Lesson 31

Lesson
31 Usage: Accept/Except, Loose/Lose, Than/Then

✏ *Words that sound alike or are spelled similarly can trap you. Don't get caught!*

....................................Did You Know?....................................

Because the following word pairs are similar in spelling and pronunciation, writers tend to confuse them. Be careful to use each word in the appropriate context.

Accept **means "to take or receive (something)" or "to consent to (something)." *Except* means "other than."**

I'd like to **accept** your invitation to address your computer club.
Any day of the week **except** Monday is all right with me.

Loose **means "not fastened" or "not tight." *Lose* means "to be unable to find" or "to fail to keep."**

The chain has come **loose** from my bicycle's back wheel.
The wheel wobbled and I started to **lose** my balance.

Than **introduces the second part of a comparison. *Then* means "at that time" or "afterward."**

New Jersey has a larger land area **than** Connecticut.
We went to Connecticut, and **then** we went to New Jersey.

Show What You Know
Underline the word in parentheses that correctly completes each sentence in the paragraphs below.

"I (accept, except) the challenge," responded the game-show contestant. "Just this one

try, and (than, then) I'll stop."

The host read the question: "What nations have more land (than, then) the U.S.? Uh-oh. I

think Rachel's microphone came (loose, lose). Let's try again. Rachel? (Buzzer.) The correct

answer is Russia, (than, then) Canada, (than, then) China. So sorry, Rachel, but you

(loose, lose). You won't get any prizes, (accept, except) the play-at-home game."

Score: _____   Total Possible: 8

62

Proofread
The following story contains words presented in this lesson. Five of them are used incorrectly. Using the proper proofreading mark, delete each incorrect word and write the correction above it.

Example: I ~~except~~ your invitation.   (accept)

One day, Lucy's pet parakeet flew away. After two weeks of looking for it, Lucy's mom

told her that she'd have to ~~except~~ (accept) her loss. "It is painful to ~~loose~~ (lose) a pet like Teresa," said Lucy

sadly. "I should never have let her loose from her cage."

~~Than~~ (Then) one day Lucy was visiting her cousin Dee in a nearby town. They heard a "tap, tap,

tap" on the kitchen window. Dee exclaimed, "I believe it's Teresa!"

Dee's mom said, "This is the wildest pet story I've ever heard."

"~~Accept~~ (Except) for Juan's snake story," suggested Dee. "Juan claimed that when his

pet snake got ~~lose~~ (loose), it came out of the wall in his neighbor's apartment!"

Practice
Write sentences for each of the word pairs presented in this lesson. Use your imagination to create interesting sentences.

Review the sentences to be sure that your child has:

• written a sentence for each lesson word.

• used each lesson word correctly in the sentence.

• written imaginative sentences that make sense and are

mechanically correct.

Tips for Your Own Writing: Proofreading..................................
Scan a piece of your writing looking for the words in this lesson. Use *then* for "next"—*than* for "compare"; *accept* for "receive"—*except* for "not"; *loose* for "not tight"—*lose* for "no win."

✏ *Accept the fact that English words are sometimes tricky to spell (except when you know all the spellings)!*

63

....

Lesson 32

Lesson
32 Usage: Principle/Principal, There/They're/Their, Its/It's

✏ *Homophones are words that sound alike but have different spellings and meanings. The words in this lesson are homophones.*

....................................Did You Know?....................................

Because the following words sound the same and look alike, writers tend to confuse them. Context is the best clue as to which word to use in a sentence.

Principle **means "a basic rule or belief." *Principal* means "most important" or "main." It also means "the chief or main person."**

This science experiment demonstrates the **principle** of inertia.
Mrs. Monetti's **principal** objection was the noise.
Mrs. Monetti is the **principal** of our school.

There **means "at that place." *They're* is a contraction for "they are." *Their* means "belonging to them."**

The people in Lake Landis really like it **there**.
They're having a wonderful festival in July.
Have you seen **their** brochure for the festival?

Its **is the possessive form of *it*. *It's* is a contraction for "it is."**

The bird fluffed up **its** feathers.
You know **it's** going to be a cold day.

Show What You Know
Underline the word in parentheses that correctly completes each sentence in the paragraph below.

Today I'll demonstrate the (principle, principal) of osmosis. (Its, It's) the

(principle, principal) lesson that we'll cover this week. Osmosis is the movement of one solution

to another when (they're, their) separated by a membrane. A plant absorbs most of (its, it's)

water by the process of osmosis. Would the lab groups please pick up (there, their) notebooks

and follow me? If you will gather around Table 2, you will see that a demonstration is set up

(there, their).

Score: _____   Total Possible: 7

64

Proofread
In Talia's report, use the proper proofreading mark to delete each of the six incorrect words and write the correction above it.

Example: They forgot ~~there~~ (their) books.

Dragonflies are among the most beautiful insects. Because their ~~principle~~ (principal) food is insects,

~~their~~ (they're) helpful, too. They can eat ~~there~~ (their) own weight in insects in a half hour.

It's hard to believe, but a dragonfly lives almost ~~its~~ (its) entire life in a wingless form called a

nymph. The beautiful, gauzy-winged flier that we know represents only a few weeks to a few

months of this insect's life. Dragonflies live for several years.

No insect can fly as fast as a dragonfly. ~~They're~~ (There) are reports of these fliers darting as fast

as a car on the highway—60 mph! No wonder they can catch so many insects.

Some extinct ancestors of today's dragonfly were huge. They

had wingspans of almost three feet. ~~Its~~ (It's) hard to imagine that!

Practice
Look at the picture. How would you react to seeing a giant dragonfly? Write a description of this dragonfly as if you were seeing it in real life. Try to use the words introduced in this lesson.

Review the description to be sure that your child has:

• used rich vocabulary (adjectives, adverbs, verbs)

to describe what he or she sees.

• written a strong description of his or her emotional response to the scene.

• written sentences that make sense and are mechanically correct.

Tips for Your Own Writing: Proofreading..................................
Search for any of these troublesome words—*principal/principle, there/they're/their, its/it's*—in a piece of your own writing. Determine whether you have used the words correctly.

✏ *Don't forget the apostrophe! It's a small mark, but its presence can make all the difference.*

65

Answer Key **137**

Lesson 33

Lesson
33 Review: Adjectives, Adverbs

A. In the following movie review, underline the correct form of the adjective in each set of parentheses.

For a really (<u>good</u>, best) film, see *Danada Square* by director George Chan. It is a
(more sentimental, sentimentaler) movie than Chan's previous film, *Run Home! Danada Square*
₂
tells the story of a young Asian-American woman who starts a business in a shopping center.
She encounters many difficulties, including prejudice. But the (baddest, <u>worst</u>) part of all her
₃
troubles is conflict with the landlord of her store. Of course, this (<u>bad</u>, worst) person is the
₄
villain of the movie. Of Chan's four films, I think that this is the (goodest, <u>best</u>) one.
₅

On the other hand, *Damage in Kuala Lumpur* is the (baddest, <u>worst</u>) movie I've seen in
₆
years. It's a disaster movie about three high-rise towers in that Asian capital. The (taller, <u>tallest</u>)
₇
of the three, called the "Black Tower," has a bomb scare. Then the "Green Tower," which is
(<u>taller</u>, tallest) than the "White Tower," catches fire. So it goes. Stay away from this movie and
₈
save your money!

Score: _____   Total Possible: 8

B. In each sentence in the paragraph below, underline the correct form of the adverb in parentheses.

Ziggy Zales hit (<u>low</u>, more low) in yesterday's opening match. He hits the
₁
(most low, <u>lowest</u>) of any tennis player that I can recall. Laura Farfone delivers the
₂
(most fast, <u>fastest</u>) serve of any tennis player. Her serve is definitely (fast, <u>faster</u>) than that of
₃   ₄
champion Maria Rivera. Some people think tennis moves (<u>more quickly</u>, quicklier) than baseball.
₅
Laura slept (<u>badly</u>, bad) before the tennis match. But Ziggy slept (more badly, <u>worse</u>) than
₆   ₇
Laura.

Score: _____   Total Possible: 7

66

C. Choose the word from the parentheses that correctly completes each sentence and write it in the blank.

1. The defense attorneys were certain that their case was very ___strong___. (strong, strongly)

2. "I ___strongly___ object!" exclaimed the lawyer. (strong, strongly)

3. The main witness for the defense related a ___sad___ story. (sad, sadly)

4. She ___sadly___ wiped her tears away, which was a nice touch. (sad, sadly)

5. The attorney wants a ___prompt___ conclusion to this trial. (prompt, promptly)

6. "The court will reconvene ___promptly___ at ten o'clock," said Judge Wu. (prompt, promptly)

Score: _____   Total Possible: 6

D. Read Marla's report on "Weird Planets." There are twelve errors. Using the proper proofreading mark, delete each incorrect word and write the correction above it.

              principal
The more we know about the ~~principle~~ planets in our solar system, the more normal our
                they're
planet Earth seems. Earth has eight planet cousins, and ~~their~~ really weird!

    Consider Mercury, the planet closest to the sun. A day on Mercury is 88 Earth days long.
                                     badly
One side of Mercury faces the sun for 88 days in a row, getting ~~bad~~ burned at 800°F. The
            lose   It's
opposite, shady side must ~~loose~~ heat for those 88 days. ~~Its~~ frigid!

                       except
Saturn is beautiful, ~~accept~~ it is deadly. It has the largest and most visible rings, which
          its   there
circle ~~it's~~ middle like a belt. You wouldn't want to vacation ~~their~~. Saturn's winds blow at speeds
                             than
of 1,000 mph. That's about five times faster ~~then~~ a severe tornado's winds.

                                          principal
But the weirdest planet is Uranus. This planet violates the ~~principle~~ by which the other
planets rotate like tops. Instead, Uranus spins oddly on its side. (If I were Uranus, I wouldn't feel
    well   accept
very ~~good~~ after eons of this motion.) Uranus should ~~except~~ the "weirdest planet" award!

Score: _____   Total Possible: 12

REVIEW SCORE: _____   REVIEW TOTAL: 33

67

Lesson 34

Lesson
34 Usage: Plural Nouns

One, two, three—how many? Two or more means "use the plural."

.................Did You Know?.................

A singular noun names one person, place, thing, or idea. A plural noun names two or more persons, places, things, or ideas.

Plural nouns are formed in the following ways:

• **most nouns, add -s.**

  girl**s** friend**s**

• **nouns ending in s, sh, ch, or x, add -es.**

  box**es** church**es**

• **nouns ending in y preceded by a consonant, change y to i and add -es.**

  bod**ies**

• **nouns ending in y preceded by a vowel, add just -s.**

  toy—toy**s** boy—boy**s**

• **some nouns ending in o, add -s. Some ending in o preceded by a consonant, add -es.**

  radio**s** echo**es**

• **many nouns ending in f or fe, change the f to v and add -es or -s. Some nouns ending in f, add only -s.**

  calf—cal**ves**
  knife—kni**ves**
  chief—chief**s**

• **a few nouns, make no change between the singular and plural.**

  sheep moose

• **a few nouns form the plural irregularly.**

  goose—geese
  child—children

Show What You Know
Write the plurals of the underlined words on the lines.

1. the <u>echo</u> of two <u>banjo</u>   echoes, banjos

2. recipe: ten ripe <u>cherry</u> and two <u>tomato</u>   cherries, tomatoes

3. some <u>essay</u> challenge your <u>belief</u>   essays, beliefs

4. the report "<u>Wolf</u> and <u>Fox</u>"   Wolves, Foxes

5. a new play, "Do <u>Sheep</u> Have <u>Tooth</u>?"   Sheep, Teeth

Score: _____   Total Possible: 10

68

Proofread
Read Dino's story. He has formed seven plurals incorrectly. Using the proper proofreading mark, delete each incorrect plural and write the correct word above it.

              stories
Example: I read three ~~storys~~ today.

        friends   computers
My ~~friendes~~ and I wanted to have a computer club. We're crazy about ~~computeres~~. We
started inviting everyone we thought would like to join. We decided not to have a president
                                         chiefs
because we don't like the idea of having bosses. Instead, we have two ~~chieves~~ a chief program
                                    vetoes   decisions
chairperson and a chief refreshment chair. They will have no ~~vetos~~ over club ~~decisiones~~.

                                                 Torpedoes
Thinking up a clever name wasn't easy. In the end, we chose "~~Torpedos~~." Why? Because
       torpedoes
sometimes ~~torpedos~~ come after you, figuratively speaking, when you carelessly key in a
mistake!

Practice
Write a brief story about an afternoon "lineup" on the radio. Include plural nouns in your writing.

Review the story to be sure that your child has:

• used the plural word forms correctly.

• included a variety of topics.

• written sentences that make sense and are mechanically correct.

_____

_____

_____

_____

Tips for Your Own Writing: Proofreading.................

If a plural form you want to use in your writing is not shown in this lesson, look the noun up in the dictionary. Most dictionaries list irregular plurals. Otherwise, add -s or -es to the noun.

Adding -s is a good bet for forming a plural, but it won't always be right.

69

Lesson 35

Lesson
35 Usage: Possessive Nouns

It's mine! It's mine! Possessive nouns show ownership.

.........................Did You Know?.........................

A **possessive noun** shows ownership of a noun that follows. Remember: a **noun** is a word that names a person, place, thing, or idea.

The following rules show how to form the possessive of nouns:

If the noun is singular, add an apostrophe and s.

I'm going to my sister**'s** new office.
Cass**'s** job is public relations director of the national fair.

If the noun is plural and ends in s, add an apostrophe only.

This national fair is the cities**'** showcase.

If the noun is plural and does not end in s, add an apostrophe and s.

The fair has a children**'s** pavilion.

Show What You Know
On the line, write the correct possessive form of each underlined noun.

1. <u>birds</u> adaptations for flight   birds'
2. a <u>bird</u> wing   bird's
3. an <u>ostrich</u> story   ostrich's
4. an <u>ibis</u> story   ibis's
5. <u>owls</u> quiet hunting flights   owls'
6. <u>mice</u> chances when a hawk is near   mice's

Score: _____   Total Possible: 6

70

Proofread
Read Marianne's report. Using the proper proofreading mark, delete each of the five incorrect possessive nouns and write the correction above it.

Example: What is your ~~cousins's~~ name? *(cousin's)*

In ancient Greece, many myths were told and later written down. One such myth is about Icarus, who was ~~Daedalus's~~ son. *(Daedalus's)* Daedalus was a marvelous builder and inventor. But he had been imprisoned in a maze for a crime. Daedalus saw a way to escape. He made wings for himself out of ~~birds's~~ *(birds')* feathers and some wax. Using the wings, Daedalus was able to fly out of the maze.

Icarus was so excited by the ~~wings's~~ *(wings')* power and the thrill of flying that he ignored his father's warning. He used his ~~fathers~~ *(father's)* wings and flew higher and higher. He got too close to the ~~suns~~ *(sun's)* burning rays and melted the wax that held together his wings. He fell to his death.

Practice
Look at the picture. Imagine that you are the rabbit and that you are being hunted by the owl. What emotions would you feel? What strategies would you devise to outwit this bird of prey? Write a paragraph of the rabbit's thoughts below. Use some possessive nouns in your paragraph.

Review the paragraph to be sure that your child has:

• used possessive nouns correctly as he or she expressed his or her emotions.

• created colorful summaries written from the rabbit's point of view.

• written sentences that make sense and are mechanically correct.

Tips for Your Own Writing: Proofreading.........................
Choose something you have written recently. Check any possessive nouns you used to make sure you have used apostrophes correctly.

You've done another day's work. Or is it two days' work?

71

Lesson 36

Lesson
36 Usage: Contractions

Here's a hint for identifying contractions: look for the apostrophe and see whether any letters have been omitted.

.........................Did You Know?.........................

A **contraction** is a word formed by combining two words and omitting one or more letters. We show the omission of letters by inserting an apostrophe. One type of contraction combines a pronoun and verb.

she + is = she's	I + am = I'm
who + is = who's	we + are = we're
I + have = I've	he + will = he'll
you + have = you've	they + will = they'll

Another type of contraction combines a verb and the negative word *not*.

are + not = aren't   will + not = won't

Do not confuse contractions with possessive pronouns. For example, the contraction *you're* sounds like the possessive pronoun *your*.

You're sorry that you lost **your** videocassette.

Show What You Know
In the paragraph below, write the contraction for each underlined word or group of words above the word or words.

We're **We are** disturbed about plans for the new superhighway. *It's* <u>It is</u> supposed to cut through the forest preserve. If the road is built, some animal populations <u>will not</u> *won't* survive. They <u>cannot</u> *can't* tolerate the increased noise and air pollution. <u>We have</u> *We've* formed a citizen committee to work for a change. <u>Who is</u> *Who's* interested in becoming a member? <u>I am</u> *I'm* in charge of next month's meeting. Please <u>do not</u> *don't* forget to sign our petition before you leave.

Score: _____   Total Possible: 8

72

Proofread
Read the following tour guide to a historic house. Help the editors make seven corrections. Using the proper proofreading mark, delete each incorrect contraction and write the correction above it.

Example: ~~Ill~~ *(I'll)* be home by dark.

Welcome to the Elisa Bentley house. ~~Wont~~ *(Won't)* you come in? ~~Youre~~ *(Your)* first stop is the vestibule, a small entry room. Notice the hand-painted wallpaper from about the 1800s. ~~Its~~ *(It's)* really quite rare. Next, ~~youll~~ *(you'll)* enter the formal parlor. Of course, this house had no electricity, and ~~weve~~ *(we've)* tried to preserve that feeling by using low lighting. Notice the Regency style of decoration. ~~Isnt~~ *(Isn't)* it exquisite! The master bedroom is next. Here ~~well~~ *(we'll)* see a hand-carved, four-poster bed. Ms. Bentley was most particular about the condition of her bed. Please return to the front of the house. Your tour has ended.

Practice
Imagine that you will write a guide for your room or some other room that you know well. Follow these steps:

1. Allow yourself time to walk through the room (at least in your mind) and notice details.
2. Decide which details are worth writing about and which ones should be left out.
3. Write the guide to the room just as if you were walking around it, noticing the details.

Review the guide to be sure that your child has:

• used any contractions correctly.

• written the information in his or her guide in a logical order.

• written sentences that make sense and are mechanically correct.

Tips for Your Own Writing: Proofreading.........................
Remember that a contraction stands for two words. It must have an apostrophe. A possessive pronoun never uses an apostrophe.

If you'll try hard, you won't fail to understand contractions.

73

Lesson 37

Lesson

37 Review: Plurals, Possessives, Contractions

A. In each sentence, form the plural of the word in parentheses and write it in the blank to complete the sentence.

1. Today's _____computers_____ have a wide variety of software. (computer)
2. Our software usually comes in _____boxes_____ that we call *packages*. (box)
3. You can play many _____games_____ on the computer. (game)
4. My screen saver shows little _____torpedoes_____ gliding through the water. (torpedo)
5. I've also seen screen savers that show _____tomatoes_____ exploding. (tomato)
6. Many people used to regard computers as _____toys_____. (toy)
7. But _____bosses_____ in offices find that software makes workers productive. (boss)
8. Software can teach you fingering for _____banjos_____ or tuning for pianos. (banjo)
9. Some do-it-yourself packages tell how to repair _____roofs_____ on houses. (roof)
10. Packages even instruct _____beginners_____ on building thermal homes. (beginner)
11. And some packages tell farmers how to raise calves and _____geese_____. (goose)
12. You could probably tell many more _____stories_____ about unusual software. (story)

Score: _____   Total Possible: 12

B. In the paragraph below, write the possessive form of each underlined word above it.

I couldn't help laughing at Dad [Dad's] accident. He dabbed red paint on both of his sleeves [sleeves'] cuffs. He "had a sheep [sheep's] face"—meaning he looked sheepish. I couldn't wait to see the kids [kids'] reaction when they came in. "It was my hands [hands'] fault," said Dad. "They're clumsy."

Score: _____   Total Possible: 5

C. Read this explanation of the naming of the computer object we call a *mouse*. If an underlined possessive or plural noun is used correctly, write C above it. Otherwise, write the correction there.

Have you wondered where computer objects' [C] names come from? A *bug* is so named because a real insect interrupted several circuits [circuits'] electron flow in an early computer. But perhaps the mouses [mouse's] name is the most humorous. It's not difficult to guess the name's [C] origin. A computers [computer's] mouse has a long "tail" and a smooth, rounded shape. How strange it would be if the computer mouse looked like a goose. Would we now have "geese-driven" [C] software programs?

Score: _____   Total Possible: 6

D. Read the following science report. It contains eight errors. Using the proper proofreading mark, delete each incorrect contraction and write the correction above it.

Large birds of prey are very territorial. This means that they wont [won't] tolerate other large birds living nearby, especially if the other birds' diets are similar to theirs. They want to avoid competition with the other birds.

Large crows and owls, for example, do not mix well. The spring is an especially tough time of year, because their [they're] trying to raise their young. If youre [you're] lucky enough to live in an uncrowded area that has many large trees, you may see this bird drama played out above you're [your] own head.

Large owls are very powerful creatures, and most birds dont [don't] bother them. But crows are very social—this means that they're accustomed to living closely with each other. And they rely on each other, too. When crows feel threatened, theyl [they'll] call all other crows within earshot. (Wer'e [We're] used to the sound of crows. They're very noisy birds.) In this way, many crows can gang up on an owl. In the end, its [it's] quite possible for the crows to win.

Score: _____   Total Possible: 8

REVIEW SCORE: _____   REVIEW TOTAL: 31

74   75

Lesson 38

Lesson

38 Usage: Simple Past Tense

"It was the best of times, it was the worst of times." How do we tell about things that happened in the past?

Did You Know?

Tenses of verbs tell whether an action or a state of being took place in the past, the present, or the future.

We use the past tense of a verb to talk or write about something that happened in the past. The simple past tense consists of one word that describes a past action. Many verbs form the simple past tense by adding *-d* or *-ed* to the present tense.

Present Tense	Simple Past Tense
Today they ask.	Yesterday they ask**ed**.
Today they play.	Yesterday they play**ed**.
Today they climb.	Yesterday they climb**ed**.

Other verbs form the simple past tense irregularly: sometimes by changing spellings, sometimes by not changing at all.

Present Tense	Simple Past Tense	Present Tense	Simple Past Tense
make	made	buy	bought
choose	chose	drink	drank
know	knew	hit	hit
feel	felt	cut	cut

Show What You Know
In the blank, write the correct past tense of the verb in parentheses to complete the sentence.

1. Clara _____decided_____ to paint her house this summer. (decide)
2. The store manager _____recommended_____ a good brand of paint. (recommend)
3. Then Clara _____bought_____ many cans of that paint. (buy)
4. Next, she _____scraped_____ the old paint off the exterior of her house. (scrape)
5. To reach the high spots, she carefully _____climbed_____ on a strong ladder. (climb)
6. Then Clara _____brushed_____ the paint on the outside walls. (brush)
7. That evening she _____admired_____ her freshly painted home. (admire)

Score: _____   Total Possible: 7

Proofread
Using the proper proofreading mark, delete each of the twelve incorrect past-tense verbs and write the correct word above it.

Example: Yesterday I was ask [asked] to a party.

Last May our town celebrated its centennial, or one-hundredth, anniversary. We maked [made] a lot of preparations. A cleanup committee wash [washed] and brush [brushed] all public buildings. Members of the fire department clumb [climbed] on high ladders to put up flags and bunting.

At last the celebration started. The high point was when Mayor Lopez ask [asked] Olga Janssen—at 105, our oldest citizen—what she rememberd [remembered] about the old days. "How I use [used] a churn to make butter and playd [played] dominoes with my cousins," said Mrs. Janssen.

At the end, we all drunk [drank] a ginger ale toast to the town's next century. We knowed [knew] most of us wouldn't be here for the next celebration, but we feeled [felt] happy to be at this one. To officially close our celebration, the mayor hitted [hit] a large bell with a mallet.

Practice
Rewrite the story in Show What You Know, describing Clara's painting experience. Add descriptive details. When the story is finished, underline all the past-tense verbs.

Review the story to be sure that your child has:

• underlined all the verbs in simple past tense, correctly identifying these verbs.

• expanded the plot of the story.

• written sentences that make sense and are mechanically correct.

Tips for Your Own Writing: Proofreading
If you need help with past-tense verbs, use the dictionary. A dictionary entry for an irregular verb usually lists the past-tense form right after the main entry. For any verbs that give you trouble, write them in your journal or writing folder where you can find them easily.

The only time you can control time is when you change verb tense!

76   77

Lesson 39

Lesson 39 Usage: Subject-Verb Agreement I

You don't want your subjects and verbs to fight with each other. Make sure they agree!

.................................Did You Know?.................................

The present **tense** form of a verb is used to talk or write about something that is happening now. In the present tense of most verbs, the only form that changes is the one used with *he, she,* or *it.* This form adds either *-s* or *-es.* By using the appropriate form of the verb with the subject, we make the subject and verb agree in number. A verb with an *-s* ending is used with *he, she, it,* or other singular subjects, and a verb without an *-s* ending is used with all other subjects.

A **conjugation** is a table of the forms that a verb takes in a particular tense. Below are conjugations of two verbs in the present tense.

Present Tense of *Live*		Present Tense of *Fix*	
I live	we live	I fix	we fix
you live	you live	you fix	you fix
he, she, it live**s**	they live	he, she, it fix**es**	they fix

Most verbs ending in *s, sh,* or *ch* add *-es* in the present form for *he, she,* or *it.*

Show What You Know

If the subject and verb in each sentence agree, put a *C* above the underlined verb. If they do not agree, write the correct present-tense form of the verb above the underlined verb.

1. My older sister Karin <u>fixes</u> cars.   *C*
2. She washes and <u>wax</u> them, too, for a small fee.   *waxes*
3. Karin <u>works</u> on cars most Saturdays.   *C*
4. She often <u>start</u> working at 7:00 in the morning.   *starts*
5. Mom isn't very good with cars, so she sometimes <u>watch</u> Karin.   *watches*
6. Karin only <u>wish</u> she could make more money fixing cars.   *wishes*
7. I think Karin is too busy. She <u>dash</u> from one thing to another.   *dashes*
8. I think she <u>try</u> to do too much between school and her job.   *tries*

Score: _____   Total Possible: 8

78

Proofread

Rick's report, entitled "How We Depend on Electricity," has five verbs and subjects that do not agree. Using the proper proofreading mark, delete the verb in each error of agreement. Above it, write the verb form that corrects the agreement problem.

Example: That dog ~~bark~~ too much.   *barks*

We often don't realize how much we depend on electricity until it ~~stop~~. When lightning   *stops*
flashes or a powerful wind ~~blow~~ down a power line, we're in trouble!   *blows*

Want to watch TV or listen to that new CD? Not without electricity. Think you'll have
some dinner? Try it cold. The family member who ~~fix~~ the food will love doing without a stove.   *fixes*
You'd like to read a book? Read while the candle ~~melt~~!   *melts*

You feel so thankful when the power ~~come~~ on again. How did   *comes*
people live without it?

Practice

Look at the picture. It shows one way family and friends entertained themselves at night before electricity. Imagine that you will have to live for a period of several weeks or months without electricity. How will you entertain yourself and others? How will you cope with the nighttime darkness? Write a short description of what you would do.

Review the description to be sure that your child has:

• used correct subject-verb agreement in each sentence.

• combined imagination with a touch of reality in his or her writing.

• written sentences that make sense and are mechanically correct.

_____

_____

_____

Tips for Your Own Writing: Proofreading

Select a piece of your own writing and look for verbs in the present tense. Check for agreement with the subject. Just remember: the verb adds *-s* or *-es* when the subject is *he, she, it,* or any singular noun.

Subjects and verbs that work together make strong sentences.

79

Lesson 40

Lesson 40 Usage: Subject-Verb Agreement II

Where's the subject? Where's the verb? If you can answer these questions, you're a long way toward understanding this lesson.

.................................Did You Know?.................................

There are some special problems of agreement between subjects and verbs. In most cases, the subject comes before the verb. However, sometimes we invert, or reverse the order of, subjects and verbs to make a sentence more interesting.

Out of the fog **rises** the **castle.**

Sentences that begin with *here, there,* and *where* put the subject after the verb.

Here **is** the **drawbridge.**
Where **are** the **gates?**

Sometimes a prepositional phrase comes between the subject and the verb.

A **knight** with many servants **arrives** at the castle.

A *compound subject* is made of two or more nouns or pronouns. Compound subjects joined by *and* always take a verb that does not end in *-s.* If the verb is irregular, use the form for plural subjects with a compound subject.

The **knight and** his **squire are** attending the tournament.

Compound subjects joined by *or* or *nor* take a form of the verb that agrees with the subject nearest to the verb.

Either the queen or **her servants have** the secret key.

Show What You Know

If the subject and verb in each sentence agree, put a *C* above the underlined verb. If they do not, write the correct present-tense form of the verb above the underlined verb.

Where <u>is</u> evidence of the Ice Age in North America? Many U.S. states and Canadian   *C* (1)
provinces <u>show</u> such evidence. Objects under a glacial mass <u>forms</u> various land features.   (2) *form* (3)
Moraines and eskers <u>are</u> types of glacial deposits. From glacial ice <u>come</u> most of the fresh   (4) *C* (5)
water on Earth. Glaciers <u>ranges</u> in thickness from 300 to 10,000 feet.   (6) *range*

Score: _____   Total Possible: 6

80

Proofread

Following is a report Tara wrote after a field trip with her science class. Find the six errors of subject-verb agreement. Using the proper proofreading mark, delete each incorrect word and write the correction above it.

Example: There ~~is~~ five science books on the table.   *are*

About twenty thousand years ago, the last glacier of the most recent Ice Age retreated
northward. As a result, many glacial formations ~~dots~~ our fertile farmlands. Everywhere ~~is~~ low   *dot*   *are*
mounds covered with trees. These mounds in each area ~~tells~~ a story. On some of them ~~grows~~   *tell*   *grow*
no crops. Farmers don't always ~~plows~~ the rougher, rockier soil of the glacial mounds. Glaciers   *plow*
have also left behind kettle lakes. A kettle is a bowl-like depression. It remains after a huge
chunk of glacial ice has melted. Terminal moraines—long, hilly ridges—also mark the end of
glaciers. You can see one if you follow Route 77 westward from Barrytown. But neither kettles
nor terminal moraines ~~tells~~ the entire story of glaciers in the Ice   *tell*
Age. For the whole story, you'll have to study geology.

Practice

Write a paragraph describing the terrain, or land formation, in your area. Is it flat, hilly, or coastal? What kind of vegetation covers the land? Be careful about subject-verb agreement.

Review the paragraph to be sure that your child has:

• used correct subject-verb agreement in his or her sentences.

• used rich vocabulary and precision of description.

• written sentences that make sense and are mechanically correct.

_____

_____

Tips for Your Own Writing: Proofreading

The next time you write a story or report, try using some compound subjects. If you join the subjects with *and,* use a verb form that does not end in *-s.* If the subjects are joined by *or* or *nor,* use a verb form that agrees with the nearest subject.

To make verbs and subjects agree, first identify the verbs and the subjects.

81

Lesson 41

Lesson
41 Review: Past Tense Verbs, Subject-Verb Agreement

A. **In the blank in each sentence, write the past tense of the verb in parentheses.**

1. Jamal's teacher ___asked___ him to perform in the piano recital. (ask)

2. He ___chose___ a piece by Chopin called "Valse Brilliante." (choose)

3. When Jamal walked onto the stage, he ___felt___ very nervous. (feel)

4. He ___remembered___ the beginning of his piece, but not the ending. (remember)

5. As Jamal ___touched___ the keys, he felt more confident. (touch)

6. He ___hit___ every single note perfectly. (hit)

7. At the reception, everyone said, "Jamal, you ___played___ very well." (play)

Score: _____ Total Possible: 7

B. **In the blank, write the correct ending (s or es) for each incomplete verb. The completed verb should agree in number with its subject.**

Tornadoes are fantastically powerful whirlwinds. A tornado form _s_ (1) along a front, or narrow zone, between a mass of cool, dry air and a mass of warm, very humid air. The warm, moist air rise _s_ (2) in rapid updrafts. Soon, a column of air spin _s_ (3). If the updraft is powerful enough, it feed _s_ (4) the growing tornado. Air rush _es_ (5) up the column.

Soon a funnel drop _s_ (6) down from the sky. It touch _es_ (7) down, raising a black dust cloud. A tornado toss _es_ (8) about debris like paper. It sometimes pitch _es_ (9) automobiles or tractors like softballs. Tornadoes would seem like pranksters if they weren't so violent. A twister sometimes levels houses on one side of a street but miss _es_ (10) those on the other side completely. The narrow, whirling column pass _es_ (11) close to some objects without harming them. Thank goodness the average tornado live _s_ (12) for only a few minutes!

Score: _____ Total Possible: 12

82

C. **In each pair of verbs in parentheses, underline the verb that agrees in number with the subject.**

Out of the shadows (step, <u>steps</u>) the king's herald. "I declare, according to His Majesty's will," he cries, "that from this day forward the queen and her retinue shall be kept under guard in the palace." Through the crowd (run, <u>runs</u>) a low murmur.

But where (<u>is</u>, are) the key to the secret passage under the palace? Does the queen have it? No, Prince Renaldo (possess, <u>possesses</u>) it. He and Princess Angelina (<u>plot</u>, plots) to aid the queen.

What is the climax of our story? The queen and her servants (makes, <u>make</u>) their escape. Neither the officials of the court nor the king (find, <u>finds</u>) a way to stop them. Into the free light and air they (<u>walk</u>, walks).

Score: _____ Total Possible: 8

D. **Fill in each blank with is, are, was, or were so that the subject and the verb agree in tense and number.**

Asteroids are rocky chunks that orbit the sun in space. Sometimes an asteroid comes into Earth's atmosphere and becomes a meteor. Usually, a meteor vaporizes in the atmosphere. We call the objects that do reach the ground *meteorites*. There ___is___ (1) evidence that meteorites have slammed into Earth. They have left very large craters. In a few cases, there ___are___ (2) surviving meteorites, too.

Meteorites can be very destructive. Scientists believe that there ___was___ (3) a huge meteorite above Siberia in 1908. It apparently exploded in the air, flattening and burning forests. Remember that there ___were___ (4) once dinosaurs on Earth. Some scientists think that a massive meteorite hit Earth and raised so much dust that it changed the climate, killing off the dinosaurs. Here ___is___ (5) something to think about: What would happen if a very large asteroid was predicted to hit Earth very soon?

Score: _____ Total Possible: 5

REVIEW SCORE: _____ REVIEW TOTAL: 32

83

....

Lesson 42

Lesson
42 Usage: Pronouns—Agreement and Order I

Be a "pro" when using the subject forms of personal pronouns.

....................Did You Know?....................

Personal pronouns have subject forms and object forms, in addition to singular, plural, and possessive forms.

The subject form of a pronoun is used as the subject of the sentence or as a pronoun following a linking verb.

A subject pronoun can be used as the subject of the sentence.

He drew the illustrations in the book.

A subject pronoun can be used after a linking verb. You can decide what form of the pronoun to use by inverting the sentence.

The author of the book was **she.**/**She** was the author of the book.

Show What You Know

Read the paragraphs. In each set of parentheses, underline the correct subject pronoun.

In 1804–1806, Captains Meriwether Lewis and William Clark led an expedition across the territory of Louisiana. Today (<u>we</u>, us) (1) know this vast region as the Northern Plains of northwestern U.S.

One woman accompanied the crew—Sacagawea. The courageous daughter of a Shoshone was (<u>she</u>, her) (2). Because Sacagawea helped with communication, the explorers were able to find horses and guides.

The explorers learned much about landforms, wildlife, and Native Americans. (<u>They</u>, Them) (3) spent their first winter in camp with the Mandan and later met the Nez Percé in the northern Rockies. Finally, in November 1805, the expedition reached the Pacific Ocean. (<u>It</u>, Its) (4) was an astonishing sight, according to Captain Clark.

Score: _____ Total Possible: 4

84

Proofread

This imaginary newspaper editorial of 1806 speculates that the members of the Lewis and Clark expedition are lost or dead. The writer used four personal pronouns incorrectly. Draw a delete mark through each mistake and write the correction above it.

Example: ~~Us~~ ^We^ have received no mail from them.

We fear that the noble expedition of Captains Lewis and Clark has failed. Consider how many conditions were against ~~they.~~ ^them^ The party was last heard from one year ago, when Corporal Warfington rowed into St. Louis. He was a member of the expedition. Since that time, ~~us~~ ^we^ have received no word. Yet our ears heard rumors of capture by Spaniards. Some think ~~them~~ ^they^ suffered an even worse fate. Whatever the truth about the noble explorers, heroes were ~~them~~ ^they^ all.

Practice

Imagine that you are a member of an exploration party in an unknown territory. Write the body of a letter to someone back home—a family member, friend, reporter, or the President. Tell a story about some challenge you have faced. Use at least four subject pronouns.

Review the letter to be sure your child has:

• written an opening and a closing. For example: the opening might say something like "We are quite well. I want to tell you what happened just yesterday."

• organized the narrative section of their letters chronologically.

• used at least four subject pronouns correctly.

Tips for Your Own Writing: Proofreading

In a piece of your own writing, check the forms of the pronouns you used. To choose the correct pronoun form, identify how the pronoun functions in each sentence. If a pronoun is used as a subject or after a linking verb, use the subject form of the pronoun.

The subject of this lesson is subject pronouns as subjects.

85

Lesson 43

Lesson
43 Usage: Pronouns—Agreement and Order II

Be clear about the uses of object pronouns: as direct objects, indirect objects, and objects of prepositions.

....................Did You Know?....................

Personal pronouns have singular and plural subject forms, object forms, and possessive forms.

An object pronoun can be used as a <u>direct object</u> of a verb. Notice that a direct object usually comes after the verb and tells what the verb acted upon.

> Because Anne's cookies are delicious, she is taking **them** to the bake sale.

An object pronoun can be used as an <u>indirect object</u> in a sentence. Notice that the indirect object comes between the verb and the direct object (*cake*). It tells to or for whom the verb acted. A direct object is necessary in a sentence with an indirect object.

> Jim bakes **her** a cake for the birthday party.

An object pronoun can be used as the <u>object of a preposition</u>. Notice that the object of a preposition comes after the preposition *for*.

> Ted and Lisa bake bread for **us**.

Show What You Know

Tell how each underlined personal pronoun is used. Is it a direct object, an indirect object, or the object of a preposition? Write DO, IO, or OP above each underlined personal pronoun.

1. "I'll splatter <u>you</u> with this pie," joked the clown. *(DO)*

2. "Go ahead, entertain <u>us</u>," dared the audience member. *(DO)*

3. "The Great Miranda" performed for <u>them</u>. *(OP)*

4. "Give <u>me</u> the ticket," said the lady at the circus box office. *(IO)*

5. Amazing Amanda the magician sawed <u>him</u> in half. *(DO)*

6. "I think we pleased <u>them</u>," said the master of ceremonies. *(DO)*

7. "We always give <u>them</u> their money's worth." *(IO)*

Score: _____ Total Possible: 7

86

Proofread

The following music review uses seven personal pronouns incorrectly. Draw a delete mark through each incorrect word and write the correction above it.

Example: Please find a seat for ~~we~~. *(us)*

The City Philharmonic played a dazzling concert last night. The conductor was pleased, and so was I. The audience agreed with ~~he~~ *(him)* and ~~I~~ *(me)*. Mellow as ever, the string section soothed and inspired ~~we~~ *(us)*. The horns blared and bounced with agility. (Give ~~they~~ *(them)* a hand!) The single brass player blasted his trumpet. (Hats off to ~~he~~ *(him)*!) But best of all, percussion player Sara Hue punctuated just the right moments. The audience gave ~~she~~ *(her)* a standing ovation! Between you and ~~I~~ *(me)*, I think it was one of the orchestra's best concerts ever.

Practice

Write five sentences describing a live performance or movie that you have attended or seen recently. It could be a concert, a sports event, a movie, or a play. Use an object pronoun in each sentence. Try to use an object pronoun as a direct object, as an indirect object, and as the object of a preposition.

Review the sentences to be sure your child has:

• used an object pronoun in each sentence.

• used the pronouns as direct object, indirect object, and object of a preposition.

_____

_____

_____

Tips for Your Own Writing: Proofreading....................

Reread something that you have written. Identify all of the personal pronouns. Did you use *It's me*? Although that is often used in informal speech, remember that the correct written form is *It is I* because *I* is the subject, not the object. *I* follows a linking verb.

The object of this lesson is to get you to put object pronouns in the right form.

87

Lesson 44

Lesson
44 Usage: Double Negatives

One negative is enough! Avoid the double negative.

....................Did You Know?....................

No, none, not, nobody, and *nothing* are negative words. Using two such negative words in the same sentence is called a *double negative*. Good writers avoid double negatives.

> **Incorrect:** I do **not** like **nothing** in my lunch box today.
> **Correct:** I do **not** like anything in my lunch box today.

> **Incorrect:** You **can't** eat **no** lunch with us.
> **Correct:** You **can't** eat any lunch with us.

The n't in *can't* stands for the negative word *not*. To avoid the double negative, watch for *not* in contractions such as *don't, won't, didn't,* and *isn't*.

The words *barely, hardly,* and *scarcely* are also used as negative words. Avoid using the negative word *not* with these words.

> **Incorrect:** I **couldn't hardly** eat after seeing that movie.
> **Correct:** I could **hardly** eat after seeing that movie.

Show What You Know

Correct each double negative that is underlined below. Rewrite the words on the line.

1. Teresa <u>couldn't do nothing</u> with her clay. *could do nothing/couldn't do anything*

2. She <u>hadn't barely</u> started sculpting class. *had barely*

3. Todd <u>didn't have no</u> clay on his table. *had no/didn't have any*

4. He <u>wasn't hardly</u> ready to get his hands dirty. *was hardly*

5. The teacher thought he <u>wouldn't never</u> get Todd to try. *wouldn't ever/would never*

6. In fact, Todd <u>wouldn't have none</u> of it. *wouldn't have any/would have none*

Score: _____ Total Possible: 6

88

Proofread

The writer of the following report has overlooked four double negatives. Draw a delete mark through each mistake and write the correction above it.

Example: I don't want ~~none~~. *(any)*

A true recycler, the hermit crab doesn't believe in ~~no~~ *(any)* waste. Because it doesn't have ~~no~~ *(any)* protective covering for its soft stomach, it goes looking for one. It ~~can't~~ *(can)* hardly wait to find an old shell. A cast-off shell from a shellfish such as a conch will do just fine. The crab pulls itself into its adopted "home." It uses tail hooks to hold the shell in place and guards the opening with crusher claws. Once it is inside, nobody ~~won't~~ *(will)* bother Mr. or Ms. Hermit Crab!

Practice

Imagine that you are writing a TV ad for a lunch food, such as the one in the picture. Write a description, or write a dialogue between two lunch items, such as a banana and a cookie. Avoid using double negatives.

Review the description to be sure your child has:

• been consistent in his or her selected approach.

(For example, if your child wrote dialogue, then he or she should use dialogue throughout.)

• avoided using any double negatives.

_____

_____

_____

_____

_____

Tips for Your Own Writing: Proofreading....................

Select a piece of your own writing. Read aloud any sentences that contain negative words. Do you hear more than one negative word in any of these sentences? Watch particularly for contractions that contain the n't.

Remember to use only one negative word in a sentence.

89

Lesson 45

Lesson
45 Review: Pronoun Agreement and Double Negatives

A. In the following article, underline the seven subject pronouns.

Maria Mitchell, the daughter of a sea captain in Nantucket, Massachusetts, lived in the 1800s. Maria helped in her father's business. He adjusted navigation instruments for oceangoing ships. They needed to be very accurate instruments. In the meantime, Maria developed an interest in astronomy. She learned how to use a telescope and studied books on astronomy in her free time.

Through careful study and observation, Maria became a very fine astronomer. On October 1, 1847, she noticed a hazy object in the sky. It was an unknown comet. Maria was the first to see it. A famous discoverer was she. Honors came to her, including a medal from the king of Denmark. Later she became professor of astronomy at Vassar College.

Score: _____ Total Possible: 7

B. In each sentence below, identify one object pronoun. If the pronoun is a direct object, draw one line under it. Draw two lines under a pronoun that is an indirect object, and circle a pronoun that is the object of a preposition.

Living things develop defenses against other living things that might eat them. Some plants use poison against their enemies to give them a nasty surprise. If you like the outdoors, poison ivy may be quite familiar to you. Oil from this plant irritates human skin, causing eruptions on it. Eating monkshood, a common garden plant, would probably kill you. But, in fact, poisonous plants can be very useful to us too. Rotenone, from a tropical plant, weakens harmful insects or kills them. Rotenone breaks down quickly in the environment and doesn't harm it. The garden plant foxglove yields a drug, digitalis. Doctors give it to heart patients.

Score: _____ Total Possible: 9

90

C. Underline five sentences with double negatives that you find in this article. Write those sentences correctly on the lines.

In 1974 a discovery was made near Xi'an (Sian) in China. This wasn't no ordinary find. Buried at the tomb of China's first emperor was a life-size army of 7,500 soldiers and horses made of terra cotta, a type of pottery. Hardly any of them weren't broken.

Archaeologists couldn't hardly believe their good luck. (An archaeologist is a scientist who studies objects from past cultures.) The creators of this "army" didn't want no one to disturb the tomb. Some figures were "booby-trapped." For example, moving a particular object may set off the release of a spear or arrow.

Would you like to see the terra-cotta army? If you think you won't never have the chance, you may be wrong. The Chinese government is allowing some of the figures to be displayed outside of China.

Samples answers are given.

This was no ordinary find.

Hardly any of them were broken.

Archaeologists could hardly believe their luck.

The creators of this army didn't want anyone to disturb the tomb.

If you think you won't ever have the chance, you may be wrong.

Score: _____ Total Possible: 5

REVIEW SCORE: _____ REVIEW TOTAL: 21

91

....

Lesson 46

Lesson
46 Grammar: Nouns

How could we speak or write without the ability to name things? Nouns are essential.

....................Did You Know?....................

A **noun** is a word that tells who or what did the action or was acted upon by the verb in the sentence.

Concrete nouns name things that you can see or touch. They can fit in the blank in this sentence: The _____ stood there.

> house   star   ice   cloth   horse   woman   child

Abstract nouns name intangible ideas or qualities—things that cannot be seen or touched.

> fairness   danger   truth   fear   love   courage   faith

A **common noun** is the general name for someone or something. A **proper noun** is the name of a particular person or place. It may consist of more than one word and begin with capital letters, except for small words such as *of*.

Common Nouns	Proper Nouns
city	Philadelphia
document	Declaration of Independence
author	Thomas Jefferson

Show What You Know
Write C or P above each underlined noun, identifying it as either a common or a proper noun. Circle any proper noun that is not capitalized.

We expect earthquakes to strike areas along the edges of continental plates. But one of the strongest earthquakes in North America struck along the mississippi river in 1811. This is right in the center of the North American plate. During and after the quake, one steamboat captain observed that the river reversed its course and ran backward. An observer in Kentucky reported that "the ground waved like a field of corn before the breeze." In northwestern Tennessee, twenty square miles of woodland sank. We know this place today as Reelfoot Lake.

Score: _____ Total Possible: 11

92

Practice
The paragraph below is missing all of its nouns. First, read the paragraph and then choose the nouns you wish to add in the blanks. Your paragraph may be serious or humorous.

Sample answers are given.

Candy is the worst taste of the century. This unnecessary and irritating mixture is produced when sugar is changed electronically. The first bar was made by mixing things such as chocolate and honey. The smell is horrible. I think I like fish better!

Revise
Read the paragraph below. Above each underlined noun, write another noun that is more specific and interesting.

Sample answers are given.

The average bee group [colony] has one important lady [queen], several hundred males, and thousands of young females called workers. By studying these workers, people [scientists] have found that bees are smart, complex, and highly social things [insects].

Worker bees have many things [jobs] to do. They clean and protect the home [hive]. They also look for juice [nectar] to make honey.

Tips for Your Own Writing: Revising
Review a piece of your writing. Look at the nouns and check to see that you chose the most specific and interesting noun you could in each case. Remember, precise word choice is an important part of effective writing.

Common nouns or proper nouns?—it's a capital difference.

93

Lesson 47

Lesson
47 Grammar: Pronouns

Pronouns take over for nouns.

...................................Did You Know?...................................

A **pronoun** is a word that takes the place of a noun or another pronoun. It keeps language from becoming repetitive.

Without Pronouns: **Heinz** wanted to make **Heinz's** best shot.
With Pronouns: **Heinz** wanted to make **his** best shot.

Pronouns can be in the first, the second, or the third person.

First person refers to the person(s) speaking.

Subject	Possessive	Object
I, we	my, our	me, us

Second person refers to the person(s) being spoken to.

Subject	Possessive	Object
you	your	you

Third person refers to a person, animal, or thing being spoken of.

Subject	Possessive	Object
he, she	his, her	him, her
it	its	it
they	their	them

The pronouns *it* and *its* refer to animals or things, never to people.

Show What You Know

Above each underlined pronoun, write *1, 2,* or *3* for first, second, or third person.

I think that Wolfgang A. Mozart was one of the greatest composers who ever lived. He
wrote an astounding number of great musical works. Opera fans especially love Mozart's
operas. One of the best of them is *The Marriage of Figaro.* In this opera, a woman tries to
regain her husband's affection. But Mozart's music is what makes this opera special. It is simply
sublime! Mozart composed orchestra and piano pieces, too. Have you ever listened to any of
his pieces?

Score: _____   Total Possible: 7

94

Proofread

Mike's story about last night's storm contains five noun repetitions that could be improved by using a pronoun. Two articles will also need to be deleted. Use the proper proofreading mark to delete each repeated noun and the two articles.

Example: Sarah rode ~~Sarah's~~ bike.
her

Hiss! Crash! Boom! So began last night's terrible thunderstorm. At about eight o'clock,
Dad was finishing up his gardening. ~~Dad~~ came running in the house and cried, "This is going _He_
to be a big one. Put the awnings down and fasten ~~the awnings.~~ ~~Awnings~~ are especially prone _them_ _They_
to wind damage."

We heard three very loud claps of thunder in a row. On the fourth, the oak tree shuddered
and split. ~~The oak tree~~ crashed to the ground. At about that time, we smelled _It_
ozone, a pungent chemical. Mom knew what this odor was, because
~~Mom's~~ major in college was meteorology, the study of weather. _her_

Practice

Write four descriptive sentences about a person you know well. You can write about a friend, parent, grandparent, or anyone you're close to. Use at least four pronouns to refer to that person. Avoid repeating nouns awkwardly.

Review the sentences to be sure your child has:

• used either a personal noun or a pronoun to refer

to the person he or she has chosen to write about.

• used at least four personal pronouns, each in the correct person and gender.

• avoided awkward noun repetition.

_____

_____

Tips for Your Own Writing: Proofreading.............

Pronouns have gender. *Masculine gender* refers to male people (*he, him, his*). *Feminine gender* refers to female people (*she, her, hers*). *Neuter gender* refers to animals or things (*it, its*). Find the pronouns in a piece of your writing. Did you use the appropriate form for each gender?

Be pro-pronoun. Use pronouns where they improve your writing.

95

Lesson 48

Lesson
48 Grammar: Verbs

Verbs are the threads that tie language together. How could we speak or write without expressing actions or states of being?

...................................Did You Know?...................................

A **verb** tells what the person, place, or thing in a sentence is doing, or it links or connects the subject to the rest of the sentence. A verb might tell about being rather than acting.

Many verbs are *action verbs.*

Hurricane gusts **whipped** the boat.
The mast of the ship **crashed** to the deck.

Linking verbs express the existence of something or link the subject with a word that renames or modifies it.

Here **is** a weather chart.   *(expresses a state of being)*
The storm **becomes** a hurricane.   *(links the subject to the renaming word)*

	Linking Verbs			
am	was	become	look	smell
is	were	feel	remain	sound
are	appear	grow	seem	taste

Some verbs can be used either as action verbs or as linking verbs.

Rena **feels** the wet grass on her bare feet.   *(action verb)*
After walking in the grass, Rena **feels** good.   *(linking verb)*

Show What You Know

Underline the verb in each sentence. Then circle each verb that is a linking verb.

Last year, we visited Uncle Taylor's turkey farm. It is quite modern. The birds dwell in
climate-controlled buildings rather than outdoors. The turkeys' claws hardly ever touch the
ground. I imagined majestic, colorful, flying birds. But these turkeys appear dull. Only plain,
white feathers cover them. Moreover, the turkeys seem quite stupid. Nevertheless, they taste
good at the Thanksgiving feast!

Score: _____   Total Possible: 13

96

Practice

Think about a ride you have enjoyed in an amusement park—a roller coaster, for example. Think of strong action verbs you might use to describe the ride or to express your emotions while on the ride. Write two sentences about the ride, using action verbs.

1. *Review sentences to be sure your child has used strong*

action verbs.

2. *Suggestions: fly, swoop, tear, rip, scream, screech,*

shake, rattle, clatter.

Now think of some linking verbs from this lesson that you might use to convey information about the ride. Write two sentences about the ride, using some of these verbs.

1. *Review sentences to be sure your child has used linking verbs.*

The sentences should convey meaningful information. One way to do this when using linking

2. *verbs is to use predicate adjectives.*

Revise

Read the paragraph below. Above each underlined verb, write another verb that is stronger and more interesting. *Sample answers are given.*

select/ choose
The Activity Club at Geller School met in September to get a name for our new
offered _suggested_
newspaper. Vance Vedder said, "The Activity Club Journal." Sandra Yee said, "The News and
debated
Doers." The club members talked for two hours. We voted three times, and each time the vote
nominated
was 4–4. Then Beth Gonzaez said, "The Geller Gazette." On the fourth vote, this name
was chosen/won
was picked.

Tips for Your Own Writing: Revising.............

Select a piece of your own writing. Identify the action verbs that you used. Then, ask yourself, "Are any of these action verbs too vague? Could they be replaced with stronger, clearer action verbs?" Think of other verbs you could use. A thesaurus may help you.

With effort and practice, you can put more verve in your verbs.

97

Lesson 49

49 Grammar: Irregular Verbs

Irregular verbs have forms of their own.

.................................Did You Know?.................................

Most English verbs are regular. Regular verbs add *-ed* to form the past tense. The past participle is formed in the same way, but it also uses a helping word such as *is, was, have,* or *had.*

> *Present*—I **walk** a lot.   *Past Tense*—I **walked** yesterday.
> *Past Participle*—I **have walked** every day.

Verbs that do not form the past and past participle by adding *-ed* are irregular verbs.

> *Present*—I **sing** a lot.   *Past Tense*—I **sang** yesterday.
> *Past Participle*—I **have sung** every day.

Present Tense	Past Tense	Past Participle	Present Tense	Past Tense	Past Participle (+ helping verb)
catch	caught	caught	make	made	made
do	did	done	ring	rang	rung
eat	ate	eaten	run	ran	run
fall	fell	fallen	speak	spoke	spoken
freeze	froze	frozen	take	took	taken
give	gave	given	teach	taught	taught
go	went	gone	throw	threw	thrown
grow	grew	grown	win	won	won

Show What You Know

Write the correct past tense form of the verb in parentheses to complete each sentence.

Beverly Sills ___grew___ up in New York City. From the time she was very young, she wanted to
1(grow)

become an opera singer. She ___began___ her operatic career in 1946. Then she joined the New
2(begin)

York City Opera in 1955. She ___became___ one of the greatest operatic sopranos of the mid-
3(become)

1900s. She ___won___ fame for her versatile voice and rich tones. Her superior abilities and warm
4(win)

personality ___made___ her popular with audiences and musicians.
5(make)

98   Score: _____   Total Possible: 5

Practice

The paragraph below is missing its verbs. In each blank, write a verb that makes sense in the sentence. Sample answers are given.

Opera is a play in which the characters ___sing___
1

their lines. It is not a drama where the characters

___read___ their lines. Opera singers must
2

___wear___ fancy costumes and ___represent___ their
3   4

roles. They may also have to ___learn___ several languages
5

and ___travel___ to other countries to study.
6

Revise

Read the paragraph below. Above the underlined words, write verbs that make sense in the story and are in the correct form. Sample answers are given.

became
Enrico Caruso got to be a famous opera singer. He first singed at Naples in 1894. Then he
                                                1
went   sang
gone to London to perform at Covent Garden. In 1903, he sanged at the Metropolitan Opera
3   4
in New York City. He had a very powerful voice. His notes rung across the stage and thrilled
                                                              5
became
audiences. He becomed one of the most famous opera stars in history.
6

Tips for Your Own Writing: Revising

Review a piece of your writing. Check the verb forms. Use these clues to see that you have used the correct forms of the verbs. Find verbs you have used and put each verb into one of these frames.

> Today I _____.   Yesterday I _____.   Tomorrow I will _____.

A dictionary can be your best friend when you need to check the forms of irregular verbs.

99

Lesson 50

50 Grammar: Adjectives

Make your nouns more interesting: modify them with adjectives.

.................................Did You Know?.................................

An **adjective** is a word that modifies a noun. *Modifies* means "describes" or "gives additional information about something."

Some adjectives tell *what kind.*

> Jamael's sister is a **brilliant** painter.

Some adjectives tell *how many.*

> The band played **many** marches for the crowd.

Some adjectives tell *which one.*

> I liked the **third** song.

Articles (*the, a, an*) are a special type of adjective, also called **determiners** because they signal that a noun follows.

> The tune is **an** old favorite.

Adjectives come before the words they modify or after a linking verb.

> The **shiny** horn blared. The drummer seems **sleepy.**

A **proper adjective** is formed from a proper noun. It is always capitalized.

> The **Italian** language is used in musical notation.

Show What You Know

Underline the adjectives (including articles) in the sentences below. Circle any proper adjectives that should be capitalized.

1. An oceanographer studies many aspects of the seas and oceans.
2. On Earth, the oceans are vast, deep pools of water.
3. But the water in oceans and seas is not drinkable.
4. It contains enormous amounts of common table salt.
5. The Pacific Ocean is the largest ocean on Earth.
6. It has many powerful currents, including the Brazil Current.

100   Score: _____   Total Possible: 19

Practice

Think of a place you like to visit—perhaps the seashore, the lake, or the desert. Close your eyes and picture the place, or a part of it. Think of six adjectives to describe it. The adjectives can describe any aspect of your mental picture—sight, sound, smell, or touch. Write the adjectives on the lines.

Review adjectives to be sure your child has used

descriptive adjectives.

Look for descriptive content (for example, *a sparkling white*

vs. *a nice beach*).

Now think of three adjectives that describe your *feelings* about this place. You can use the sentence form "I feel . . ." to express these feelings. Write the sentence on the lines.

Review adjectives to be sure your child has used descriptive adjectives.

Look for descriptive content (for example, *peaceful* vs. *happy*).

Revise

Revise the paragraph below by adding at least seven adjectives to give more details and make the picture clearer and more interesting to the reader. Write the adjectives above the nouns they modify.

Sample answers are given.
                hot, brilliant   white
The sun shone on the beach and warmed the sand. Waves splashed back and forth across
little   rippling small, red
the cove. Light sparkled on the waves. A boat sailed past in the distance. With a snort, a scuba
                                    wooden   fast
diver rose suddenly to the surface by the pier. People played a game of volleyball at one end of
crowded   huge   many interesting
the beach while children made sand castles at the other end. The sights, sounds, and smells of
                        best
the beach made it the place to be.

Tips for Your Own Writing: Revising

Choose a piece that you have written. Identify the adjectives that you used. Did you use adjectives like *good, bad,* or *nice* when you might have used a more descriptive adjective? Replace any adjectives that do not give enough detail.

Adjectives help people see the world as a colorful, interesting place.

101

---

146 Answer Key

Lesson 51

Lesson
51 Grammar: Articles

*K*now your articles: the, an, and a.

......................Did You Know?......................

Articles are special adjectives that are used only with nouns. They are also called determiners because they signal that a noun follows.

The definite article *the* **is used with a noun when the noun refers to a particular thing.**

The Olympic swimmer now speaks at schools.

The indefinite articles *a* **and** *an* **are used with a noun when the noun refers to no particular thing.**

We heard **a** swimmer speak about careers in sports.
Next week **an** acrobat will talk to us.

The article *a* **is used before a word that begins with a consonant sound:** *a* **speech.**

The article *an* **is used before a word that begins with a vowel sound:** *an* **audience.**

....

Show What You Know

Fill in each blank with the appropriate article: *the, an,* **or** *a.*

Jacques Cousteau was ___an___ important ocean explorer of this century. He made
_____1_____

many contributions to oceanography, ___the___ science of oceans. Cousteau developed
_____2_____

oxygen tanks for diving. Before divers had these tanks, they had to wear very heavy, awkward

suits. Cousteau's contribution was, therefore, ___a___ very important one. Cousteau studied
_____3_____

ocean plants and animals that are almost unknown. He also explored shipwrecks. One of

Cousteau's major concerns was pollution. He opposed ___the___ French government for
_____4_____

dumping nuclear wastes at sea.

It is not ___an___ exaggeration to say that Jacques Cousteau popularized oceanography.
_____5_____

His TV specials made millions more aware of ___the___ earth's oceans.
_____6_____

Score: _____   Total Possible: 6

102

Proofread

Gerry's report on whale music has six mistakes in its use of articles. Use the proper proofreading mark to correct each mistake.

                    an
Example: I had ⟨a⟩apple for lunch.

              an   an
Whales communicate by ⟨a⟩astonishingly rich language. They often use ⟨a⟩area of the deep

sea called the sound channel to send their sound messages over very long distances. We're not

     a   a
sure what all the whale sounds mean. But whales are known to respond to calls for help from

    a   a
⟨an⟩ great distance. Scientists wonder whether the sounds are produced on ⟨an⟩hourly or daily

schedule of some kind.

In fact, whales seem to produce two distinct groups of sounds. One group includes low-

pitched barks, whistles, screams, and moans that humans can hear. Whales also make another

                     a
group of sounds at ⟨an⟩ high frequency, or pitch, which humans cannot hear.

                                   a
Whales may use these clicks or squeaks like ⟨an⟩ kind of radar.

Perhaps they locate prey or orient themselves using these

sounds.

Practice

Look at the picture. Write three sentences to describe what is happening. Try to use the articles *the* **and** *a* **at least one time each.**

1. ___Review the sentences to be sure your child has:___
    - ___written three complete sentences.___

2. ___• used the articles the and a at least one time each.___
    - ___• described whales playfully in the water.___

3. _____

Tips for Your Own Writing: Proofreading..............

Choose a piece of your own writing. To check that you used the appropriate article with each noun, read your writing aloud. Listening to the beginning sound of each noun will help you know whether you chose the right article.

*W*hat an article! You needed the articles a, an, and the to complete the lessons.

103

Lesson 52

Lesson
52 Grammar: Adverbs

*M*ake your verbs, adjectives, and adverbs more interesting: use adverbs.

......................Did You Know?......................

An adverb is a word that modifies a verb, an adjective, or another adverb. We form many adverbs by adding *-ly* **to an adjective. We often change a final** *y* **to** *i* **before adding the** *-ly.*

quick + -ly = quickly
happy + -ly = happily

When adverbs are used with verbs, they tell *how, when, where,* **or** *to what extent.*

Brae walked **hurriedly** to the mailbox.
She slammed the door **afterward.**
Then she stomped **upstairs.**
Now Brae relaxed **completely.**

Adverbs that tell *to what extent* **can also modify adjectives and other adverbs.**

Arturo's house was **almost** invisible.
But now the fog is lifting **very** rapidly.

....

Show What You Know

Underline each adverb in the article. Draw a line to the word that each adverb modifies.

Listen carefully. You can play a violin correctly. First, hold the instrument securely against

the neck and under the chin. Take the bow firmly in the free hand. Apply the bow to the

strings so that it barely touches them. Then pull the bow evenly. Do this without breaking

contact with the strings. When you very nearly reach the end of the arc, reverse the direction

of the bow. Now you push it. The sound you hear may be rather scratchy. But remember,

learning to play the violin means practicing regularly.

Score: _____   Total Possible: 22

104

Practice

Write an adverb in each blank in the paragraph. Choose adverbs that tell about the actions of marching bands. Sample answers are given.

The bass drum ___quickly___ announced the
_____1_____

start of the parade. The beat of the snare drums

signaled the steady, rhythmical pace. The first band

played ___smartly___ as it marched ___precisely___
_____2_____   _____3_____

along the route. Everyone clapped ___loudly___
_____4_____

as the trumpets and trombones blared. The whole town ___proudly___ cheered as the magnificent cars
_____5_____

and floats traveled ___slowly___ along the parade route.
_____6_____

Revise

Revise the paragraph below by adding at least four adverbs to give more details and make the picture clearer and more interesting to the reader. Insert carets to show where the adverbs should be added. Sample answers are given.

                    slowly
Example: Beat the drum ⋀.

                                            carefully
Create your own orchestra. Find some empty pop bottles. Fill them ⋀with

              softly
water at different levels. To "play" them, blow⋀across their tops. Take a jar with a lid. Put some

                              tightly
dried beans in the jar and close the lid⋀. Shake the jar to make a rhythmic sound. Find some old

                                      briskly
metal pots and pans and a clean paintbrush. Invert the pans and "play" them⋀with the brush,

                   really
like a snare drum. If you want to get⋀fancy, make your own set of wind chimes. Use sticks,

                                      easily
string, and small pieces of metal for the "chimes." You can⋀make your own music.

Tips for Your Own Writing: Proofreading..............

Select something from your own writing and find the adverbs. Be sure that you did not use too many adverbs in any one place, as in this sentence: *I read a very, extremely, unbelievably long book.* Like adjectives, adverbs should be used with restraint.

*H*ere is very useful advice: write quite descriptively with adverbs.

105

Answer Key **147**

Lesson 53

Lesson 53 Grammar: Conjunctions and Interjections

Use conjunctions to connect words or word groups. Use interjections to express emotion.

Did You Know?

A **conjunction** is a word that connects words or groups of words.

Coordinating conjunctions such as *and, but,* and *or* connect related words, groups of words, or sentences.

Meiko **and** Bob go to dance class together.
The recital was entertaining **but** long.
Bob danced in the first dance **and** in the finale.
Meiko forgot the step, **or** her foot slipped.

Correlative conjunctions are conjunctions used in pairs to connect sentence parts.

Neither Tessa **nor** Kato wanted to be first in the lineup.
Trini had to decide **whether** to dance **or** to study piano.
We saw **both** Sharon **and** Quinn in the jazz dance.

An **interjection** is a word or words that express emotion.

Wow! Your performance in the dance recital was stupendous.
Oh, I want to learn how to dance.

Use either an exclamation point or a comma after an interjection. If the emotion being expressed is strong, use the exclamation point.

Show What You Know

Circle each conjunction and underline each interjection in the paragraph below.

Suddenly I heard, "Yipe! It's a big *snake*." The poor snake simply wanted peace and quiet. It neither rattled nor hissed. It quietly uncoiled, and then it slithered away. I wanted to follow the snake, but Terri told me to stay away from it. "Look out!" she said. "It's gone under that rock." Both Dr. Herkimer and I are snake scientists. Oh and we are both afraid of snakes!

Score: _____ Total Possible: 11

106

Practice

Look at the picture of a dog show. Write three sentences that describe the scene. Use conjunctions in at least two of the sentences, perhaps to compare and contrast the owners and their dogs. (Name them if you would like.)

1. _____ Review sentences to be sure your child has:
   • written three complete sentences.
   • used conjunctions in at least two of the
2. _____ sentences.
   • used correlative conjunctions for comparison
   and contrast.

3. _____

_____

Revise

Revise the paragraphs below by adding at least four conjunctions and one interjection to improve the writing. Use proper proofreading marks. *Samples answers are given.*

Example: We called her. We waited for her.
          and

Susan ran home from school. She was very excited. She raced in the front door. She
          as
looked for her parents. As soon as she saw her father, she yelled, "I won."
          Dad!
Goodness!
"Calm down," said Mr. Campbell. "Tell us what you won."

Susan reported that she had won first place in the science fair. She had gotten a trophy.
          and
She had gotten a medal.

Mrs. Campbell congratulated Susan. She hugged Susan. Mrs. Campbell cried. She did not
          and   *but*
cry long. Mr. Campbell smiled a lot. He told Susan they were very proud of her.
          and

Tips for Your Own Writing: Revising

Choose a piece of your own writing. Did you use any interjections? If so, did you use them only occasionally? Using too many interjections is like the boy who cried "Wolf!" too often. After a while, the excitement wears off. Save interjections for special occasions.

Wow! Conjunctions and interjections in the same lesson.

107

Lesson 54

Lesson 54 Grammar: Prepositions

Use prepositional phrases to modify words in sentences.

Did You Know?

A **preposition** connects a noun or pronoun to the rest of the sentence. The noun or pronoun that follows the preposition is called the **object of the preposition.**

The object, along with the preposition, its object, and any words that modify the object, make up a *prepositional phrase.* This phrase gives more information about the sentence.

We glanced *across* the treacherous river.

A prepositional phrase modifies a noun, pronoun, verb, adjective, or adverb. In the first sentence, the prepositional phrase *along the beach* is an *adverb phrase* that modifies the verb *walked.* In the second sentence, the prepositional phrase *along the beach* is an *adjective phrase* that modifies the noun *walk.*

We walked *along the beach.*
Our walk *along the beach* was enjoyable.

Prepositions				
about	before	down	of	to
above	behind	for	on	under
across	below	from	over	up
after	beneath	in	since	with
against	beside	like	through	without

Show What You Know

Underline each prepositional phrase. Circle the preposition.

Sweat was running down Matt's face. He couldn't believe that his opponent Marvin would clobber him, even though Marvin was champion of the school district. "Fifteen-love. Thirty-love." The scores were announced over the speaker! Matt tried to remember all he'd been taught: grip the end of the racket, but not too tightly. Stay limber and don't stand in one spot. Keep eyes on the ball. Now a serve was coming across the net. Matt crossed his fingers.

Score: _____ Total Possible: 14

108

Practice

Think of the sights, sounds, feelings, and smells of a storm. It could be a snowstorm, thunderstorm, or hurricane. Write a sentence or poem using as many prepositional phrases as you can.

Example: Rain *from the dark clouds in the sky* pounded *on the roof of the house* and pelted the trees *in the yard* as the lightning flashed *across the sky.*

Possible beginnings:
Over the trees in the yard
In the dark of night

_____ Review the poem or sentence to be sure your child has used many
prepositional phrases and has written descriptively about some of his or her sensory
perceptions—sight, sound, feeling, smell.

_____

_____

Revise

Revise the paragraph below by adding at least four prepositional phrases to provide details about the heat, the drought, or the rainy season. Use proper proofreading marks.
Samples answers are given.
          In the evening,   under the beautiful elm tree
Example: We sat outside.
          In the summer   *Under a blue sky*
Hot, dry winds sweep across much of southern Asia. The sun bakes the earth, and crops
          in the dry ground   *with great eagerness*
cannot grow. The people wait for the rainy season. The coming of the rain means that they
          in their fields   *for their families*
can plant crops and produce food.

Tips for Your Own Writing: Revising

Choose a piece that you have written recently. Look for places to add prepositional phrases to provide additional information or add interesting details to your sentences. Always try to place each phrase next to the word it modifies.

Prepositions add details to your writing.

109

Lesson 55

Lesson 55 Review: Parts of Speech

A. Underline the four proper nouns in the article below.

<u>Lucille Ball</u> was one of the most successful comedians of all time. She and her husband, <u>Desi Arnaz</u>, created an incredibly popular TV show in the 1950s. It featured their <u>New York</u> apartment and best friend, "<u>Ethel Mertz</u>."

Score: _____ Total Possible: 4

B. Write a pronoun from the list that best completes each sentence.

you   her   them   we

1. Marla twisted ____her____ ankle on the ice yesterday.
2. Ben and Rae have won the skating match. Let's congratulate ____them____.
3. Can ____we____ join our teams together to put on a bigger skating show?
4. "I know ____you____ will like skating as much as I do," said the champ to her son.

Score: _____ Total Possible: 4

C. Above each underlined verb, write A if it is an action verb and L if it is a linking verb.

1. Beavers <u>build</u> lodges in artificial lakes. [A]
2. A lodge <u>is</u> a mound of sticks with an interior chamber. [L]
3. As for the artificial lake, the beaver <u>creates</u> that by damming a stream. [A]
4. It <u>seems</u> strange that a beaver <u>can make</u> such a difference. [L] [A]

Score: _____ Total Possible: 5

D. Underline fourteen adjectives (including articles) in the report below. Circle one proper adjective.

Pluto is <u>the</u> <u>last</u> planet revolving around <u>the</u> sun. It was discovered in 1930 by (American) astronomer Clyde Tombaugh. Before <u>this</u> <u>important</u> discovery, astronomers suspected <u>the</u> existence of <u>a</u> <u>ninth</u> planet. They had noticed that <u>a</u> force seemed to pull <u>the</u> <u>seventh</u> planet, Uranus, and <u>the</u> <u>eighth</u> planet, Neptune, off their orbits.

Score: _____ Total Possible: 15

110

E. Fill in each blank with the appropriate article: the, an, or a.

1. Find ___a___ player to pluck the banjo.
2. If you play the harp, then find ___an___ orchestra to play in.
3. This is ___the___ guitar that I played in the concert last year.

Score: _____ Total Possible: 3

F. Underline the adverb in each of the three sentences below.

1. Charles Dickens wrote <u>often</u> about children's hardships.
2. Mrs. Havisham trains Estella to treat all men <u>cruelly</u>.
3. Do you know this story <u>well</u>? It is Dickens's *Great Expectations*.

Score: _____ Total Possible: 3

G. Underline eight conjunctions and circle two interjections.

Have you ever experienced a partial or total eclipse of the sun? (Oh, my!) It's an exciting experience. The moon passes between the sun <u>and</u> Earth. It casts a shadow on Earth. <u>Not only</u> does the sky darken, <u>but also</u> the air chills. (Wow!) It feels just like nightfall!! <u>Both</u> before <u>and</u> after the deepest part of the eclipse, you have to be careful not to look directly at the sun. To do so could injure your eyes. <u>Whether</u> the eclipse is total <u>or</u> partial, a solar eclipse is something to remember.

Score: _____ Total Possible: 10

H. Underline five prepositional phrases below. Above the phrase, write the part of speech that it modifies (noun, verb, adjective).

1. Bread is a staple food <u>for many people</u>. [noun]
2. Much of the flour used to make bread comes <u>from wheat</u>. [verb]
3. The wheat heads <u>on the stalk tip</u> provide flour's raw material. [noun]
4. To harvest wheat, machines beat the heads <u>against a hard surface</u>. [verb]
5. The grain is then milled <u>into flour</u>. [verb]

Score: _____ Total Possible: 10

REVIEW SCORE: _____ REVIEW TOTAL: 54

111

Lesson 56

Lesson 56 Grammar: Combining Sentences I

You can form compound sentences in more than one way.

Did You Know?

Using compounds to combine short sentences can lead to smoother, less choppy writing.

When sentences have the same subject and verb, you can combine them easily.

Darryl eats apples.   Darryl eats plums.
Darryl eats **apples and plums.**

When two sentences have the same subject but different verbs and objects, they can also be combined.

Heather plays soccer.   Heather writes poetry.
Heather **plays soccer and writes poetry.**

Sentences with the same verb and object but different subjects can also be combined. Many times the form of the verb will change when it becomes plural.

Diehl goes to summer camp.   Timothy goes to summer camp.
Diehl and Timothy go to summer camp.

If *I* is one subject in a compound subject, it always comes *last.*

Timothy and I go to summer camp.

Show What You Know

Combine each pair of sentences into one compound sentence.

1. England is in the British Isles. Scotland is in the British Isles.
   England and Scotland are in the British Isles.

2. Aunt Tillie visited England. Aunt Tillie visited Scotland.
   Aunt Tillie visited England and Scotland.

3. She climbed mountains in Scotland. She visited gardens in England.
   She climbed mountains in Scotland and visited gardens in England.

4. Tillie sipped tea in the afternoon. Tillie ate scones in the afternoon.
   Tillie sipped tea and ate scones in the afternoon.

Score: _____ Total Possible: 4

112

Practice

Make a personal profile. First, list four of your physical characteristics such as hairstyle or color, height, and eye color. Next, list four foods that you like. Finally, list four things that you like to do for fun.

Physical Characteristics

_____   _____

_____   _____

Favorite Foods

_____   _____

_____   _____

Things I Like to Do

_____   _____

_____   _____

Using the information above, write two compound sentences telling about yourself.

1. Review sentences to be sure your child has written two complete compound sentences
   (e.g., compound subjects, compound objects, or compound predicates, i.e., verbs).

2. _____

Revise

Revise the paragraph below by rewriting at least two sentences as compound sentences. Use proper proofreading marks. Sample answers are given.

                                  and dogs
Example: Cats are mammals. ~~Dogs are mammals too.~~

                                              and crocodiles
Alligators belong to the family *Crocodylidae*. ~~Crocodiles belong to that family,~~ too. They
                      but
look a lot alike. ~~Some~~ of the crocodiles' bottom teeth show when they close their mouths.

Alligators' teeth are hidden when they close their mouths. Also, crocodiles have narrow
              and
snouts. ~~Alligators~~ have broad snouts.

Tips for Your Own Writing: Revising

Choose a piece of your own writing. Look for short, choppy sentences and see whether combining them will improve your writing. Also, look for sentences that are too long. Sometimes a very long sentence should be divided into two shorter sentences.

Be a joiner! Combine sentences whenever appropriate.

113

Lesson 57

Lesson 57 Grammar: Combining Sentences II

Do two sentences have some words in common? You may be able to combine the sentences by using an appositive.

..................................Did You Know?..................................

Sometimes we can combine two sentences by taking information from one sentence and attaching it to a closely related noun or a phrase in another sentence. Information that is "attached" in this way is called an *appositive*. If it is at the beginning or end of a sentence, you need only one comma after it or before it.

> A river always has a mouth. A mouth is the place where it flows into a larger body of water.
> A river always has a mouth, **the place where it flows into a larger body of water.**

When an appositive adds information but is not necessary to establish the meaning of the sentence, set it off with commas. Delete the appositive and see whether the sentence has the same meaning.

> Our swimming coach teaches summer school. Mrs. Santos is our swimming coach.
> Mrs. Santos, **our swimming coach,** teaches summer school.

When an appositive is needed to clarify something, do *not* use commas.

> Rube and Lou played baseball tonight. Rube and Lou are Hornets team members.
> Hornets team members **Rube and Lou** played baseball tonight.

Show What You Know
Use an appositive to combine each pair of sentences below.

1. Every country has a capital. A capital is a city where government is run.
   Every country has a capital, a city where government is run.

2. Rome is full of ancient buildings. Rome is the capital of Italy.
   Rome, the capital of Italy, is full of ancient buildings.

3. A small town is near Rome. The town has many ruins.
   A small town near Rome has many ruins.

Score: _____ Total Possible: 3

114

Practice
Look at the picture of a large public building. What adjectives does it bring to mind? Write four sentences with appositives about this building or a large public building in your own community (a local museum, for example). Include some descriptive details to help your reader visualize the building.

1. _____ Review sentences to be sure your child has:
   • written about the picture or a public building in his or
2. _____ her community.
   • written complete sentences with proper end marks.
3. _____ • included some good descriptive details.

4. _____

Revise
Revise the paragraph below. Use proper proofreading marks to combine at least two of the sentences by using appositives. Sample answers are given.

our longest street
Example: High Street has a lot of trees. It is our longest street.

the largest city in the United States,
New York City has more than seven and a half million people. It is the largest city in the
Home of the United Nations,
United States. It is one of the largest cities in the world. Only Tokyo, Japan, is larger. New York
is an important center for business, culture, and trade. It is also the home of the United
Nations. The city has banks, stock exchanges, and other financial institutions. These institutions
are located in the famous Wall Street area of the city. The Statue of Liberty is one of New
York's most well-known historic sites. It is visited by thousands of people every year.
Review sentences to be sure your child has combined sentences using appositives whenever possible.

Tips for Your Own Writing: Revising..................................
Select and reread a piece of your own writing. Are there any sentences you could combine by using an appositive? Combining information into one sentence will eliminate short, choppy sentences.

When two sentences have a lot in common, they may want to join together.

115

Lesson 58

Lesson 58 Grammar: Combining Sentences III

Do two sentences have related ideas? Are they of equal importance? If the answer to these questions is yes, you may want to form compound sentences.

..................................Did You Know?..................................

Similar sentences can be combined when they have closely related ideas of equal importance. We can form such compound sentences by using the coordinating conjunctions *and, but,* or *or.* Place a comma after the first sentence and before the conjunction.

Use *and* to join sentences that have equal importance and similar ideas.

> Mr. Raeford will bake pies. Ms. Tasco will prepare salads.
> Mr. Raeford will bake pies, **and** Ms. Tasco will prepare salads.

Use *but* to join sentences that have equal importance and contrasting ideas.

> We had a picnic on Memorial Day. We stayed indoors on Independence Day.
> We had a picnic on Memorial Day, **but** we stayed indoors on Independence Day.

Use *or* to join sentences that have equal importance and that offer a choice.

> Play games with the children. Talk to the adults.
> Play games with the children, **or** talk to the adults.

Show What You Know
Use *and, but,* or *or* to form a compound sentence from each pair of sentences. Make sure you punctuate the sentences correctly.

1. We make homemade ice cream. Our neighbors enjoy sharing it with us.
   We make homemade ice cream, and our neighbors enjoy sharing it with us.

2. I like pistachio ice cream. My sister prefers strawberry ice cream.
   I like pistachio ice cream, but my sister prefers strawberry.

3. You can have homemade ice cream with us. You can go to the movie with them.
   You can have homemade ice cream with us, or you can go to the movie with them.

Score: _____ Total Possible: 3

116

Practice
Think of holiday parties that your family has. Many families have celebrations at Thanksgiving or the Fourth of July. Use one of your family's special holiday celebrations in this writing assignment.

Write three sentences to describe the holiday celebration. Try to use each of the conjunctions *and, but,* and *or* at least one time.

1. _____ Review sentences to be sure your child has:
   • written about a holiday celebration.
   • written complete sentences with proper end
2. _____ punctuation.
   • used *and, but,* and *or* at least one time each in the sentences.
3. _____

Revise
Revise the paragraph below by combining at least two sentences. Use proper proofreading marks to add the conjunctions *and, but,* and *or.* Sample answers are given.

but
Example: I like toppings on my ice cream. My brother doesn't.

Ice cream is made from milk products, sugar, and flavorings. It is a popular dairy treat. Ice
or
cream is eaten alone. It can also be eaten with cake or pie. It is the main ingredient in milk
and
shakes, sodas, and sundaes. The most popular flavor is vanilla. Chocolate is the next most
but
popular flavor. Ice cream can be found in many parts of the world. Americans eat more ice
cream than people in any other country.

Tips for Your Own Writing: Revising..................................
Select a piece of your own writing. Did you use the conjunctions *and, but,* and *or* to join sentences that have similar ideas? If the sentences do not have similar ideas, then you should not try to combine them.

When two sentences have a lot in common, they may belong together as one.

117

Lesson 59

Lesson 59 Grammar: Combining Sentences IV

When combining sentences, use any and all methods you can. Often, there is more than one good way to combine sentences.

Did You Know?

A big part of the writer's job is *selection*, that is, deciding which details to include (and which ones to leave out).

There is more than one way to combine the following sentences.

> Mom just planted that rosebush.
> The rosebush was full of blossoms.
> We cut the rose.
> The rose smelled very fragrant.
> The rose had a bright red color.

> We cut the bright red, fragrant rose from Mom's new rosebush, which was full of blossoms.

You could also write:

> Planted recently by Mom, the rosebush yielded a bright red, fragrant rose, which we cut.

Show What You Know

Combine each set of sentences to create a new sentence. Write the new sentence on the line.
Sample answers are given.

1. I recently read a new book.   Elbert Baze wrote it.
The book is *Dinosaur Music.*   It is an entertaining book.
> I recently read an entertaining new book, *Dinosaur Music*, by Elbert Baze.

2. I didn't know that the book signing was scheduled for Tuesday.
I made other plans with Bert and Ernie.
> Not knowing that the book signing was scheduled for Tuesday, I made other plans with Bert and Ernie.

Score: _____   Total Possible: 2

118

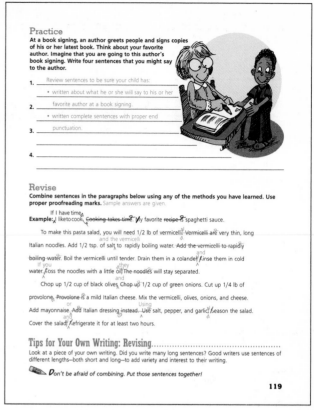

Practice

At a book signing, an author greets people and signs copies of his or her latest book. Think about your favorite author. Imagine that you are going to this author's book signing. Write four sentences that you might say to the author.

1. _____
Review sentences to be sure your child has:
• written about what he or she will say to his or her

2. _____
favorite author at a book signing

• written complete sentences with proper end

3. _____
punctuation.

4. _____

Revise

Combine sentences in the paragraphs below using any of the methods you have learned. Use proper proofreading marks. Sample answers are given.

Example: ~~I like to cook.~~ ~~Cooking takes time.~~ My favorite ~~recipe~~ is spaghetti sauce.
If I have time,

To make this pasta salad, you will need 1/2 lb of vermicelli. ~~Vermicelli are~~ very thin, long
and the vermicelli
Italian noodles. Add 1/2 tsp. of salt to rapidly boiling water. ~~Add the vermicelli to rapidly~~
and
~~boiling water.~~ Boil the vermicelli until tender. Drain them in a colander. ~~Rinse~~ them in cold
If you   they
water. ~~Toss~~ the noodles with a little oil. ~~The noodles~~ will stay separated.
and
Chop up 1/2 cup of black olives. ~~Chop up~~ 1/2 cup of green onions. Cut up 1/4 lb of
or
provolone. ~~Provolone is~~ a mild Italian cheese. Mix the vermicelli, olives, onions, and cheese.
or   Using
Add mayonnaise. ~~Add~~ Italian dressing ~~instead.~~ ~~Use~~ salt, pepper, and garlic. ~~Season~~ the salad.
and
Cover the salad. ~~Refrigerate~~ it for at least two hours.

Tips for Your Own Writing: Revising

Look at a piece of your own writing. Did you write many long sentences? Good writers use sentences of different lengths—both short and long—to add variety and interest to their writing.

Don't be afraid of combining. Put those sentences together!

119

···

Lesson 60

Lesson 60 Review: Understanding and Combining Sentences

A. Choose a word or phrase from each column to build a sentence that makes sense. Using this method, make three sentences and write them on the lines.

Subject	Verb	Object	Preposition	Object
Benny	likes	the letters	in	her aunt
We	planted	sunshine	to	the clay pot
Courtney	mailed	a flower	for	the summer

1. ____ Review sentences to be sure your child has chosen a word or phrase from each column, written
2. ____ complete sentences with correct punctuation, and written sentences that make sense. Possible
3. ____ answers: Benny planted a flower in the clay pot. We mailed the letters to her aunt. Courtney
likes sunshine in the summer.

Score: _____   Total Possible: 3

B. Combine the sentences using *and, but,* or *or.* Write the sentences on the lines.

1. Oranges have vitamin C. Grapefruits have vitamin C.
> Oranges and grapefruits have vitamin C.

2. Go camping with Gene. Go to the movies with Leslie.
> Go camping with Gene, or go to the movies with Leslie.

3. We go to the movies frequently. We often see Leslie there.
> We go to the movies frequently, and we often see Leslie there.

Score: _____   Total Possible: 3

C. Combine the following sentences, using an appositive. Write the sentence on the line.

Mrs. Tanaka is our librarian.   Mrs. Tanaka helps us with our research papers.
> Mrs. Tanaka, our librarian, helps us with our research papers.

Score: _____   Total Possible: 1

120

D. In each sentence, underline the subordinate clause and circle the main clause.

1. If you like my model ship, (I'll make you one)

2. (I think I can build it myself) unless the kit is very complicated.

Score: _____   Total Possible: 4

E. Build a sentence using the provided sentence parts. Write the sentence on the line.

the green butterfly made a comeback   no one had seen in years   which
> The green butterfly, which no one had seen in years, made a comeback.

Score: _____   Total Possible: 1

F. Combine the sentences using a participial phrase.

June was feeling sick.   June lay down and closed her eyes.
> Feeling sick, June lay down and closed her eyes.

Score: _____   Total Possible: 1

G. Combine the three sentences. Write the combined sentence on the line.
Sample answer is given.

1. Berne is a new student.   **2.** He has red hair.   **3.** Berne is good at swimming.
> Berne, the new student with red hair, is good at swimming.

Score: _____   Total Possible: 1

H. Decide whether each sentence is a statement, question, exclamation, or request. Then write the correct punctuation on the line.

1. What time does Reeva get home from work this evening ____ ?

2. Last night Janice got home at 8:30 ____ .

3. Don't stay out too late ____ .

Score: _____   Total Possible: 3

REVIEW SCORE: _____   REVIEW TOTAL: 17

121

NOTES

NOTES

NOTES

NOTES

NOTES